# YOUR TURN TO
# RISE

**12 Breakthrough strategies for Woman in the Workplace**

**BIDISHA BANERJEE**

# CONTENTS

Contents

# WHY WE RISE?

In June 2023, a headline in *Fortune Magazine* caught my eye: *"Women CEOs now run 10.4% of Fortune 500 companies. A quarter of these 52 leaders took the helm just last year."* This statement is a snapshot of progress, a brief glimpse into the ongoing journey of women in the professional world. But this journey is layered, complex, and far from over. The rise in numbers is promising, yet it serves as a reminder of the road still ahead—the road that began with the very first women stepping into workplaces.

Let's rewind and start from the beginning, the first step in what would become a marathon rather than a sprint. At the start of the 20th century, the world of work was starkly different for women. Opportunities were narrowly defined and largely restricted to roles like teaching, nursing, and domestic work. These professions were seen as natural extensions of women's roles in the home, defined by a mix of societal expectations and legal boundaries that left little room for ambition outside these parameters.

Then came World War II, a period that would dramatically shift the professional world for women. As men marched off to war, women stepped into the breach, taking on roles traditionally reserved for their male counterparts. They worked in factories, shipyards, and other critical industries, symbolized by the iconic image of "Rosie the Riveter" with her flexed arm and a steadfast gaze, capturing women's resilience and capability. Yet, this progress faced a setback when the war ended, and societal expectations nudged women back toward domestic life.

The winds of change picked up again with the rise of feminism in the 1960's and 1970s. It was a time of challenging the status quo and vehemently advocating for equal rights. Legislative changes like the Equal Pay Act of 1963 and the Civil Rights Act of 1964 in the United States began addressing workplace discrimination head-on. This era marked a significant push forward, with women breaking into professions once dominated exclusively by men, such as law, medicine, and business.

However, the journey was far from over. As we entered the 1980's and 1990s, the term "glass ceiling" came into play, describing the unseen yet unbreachable barrier that kept women from reaching the upper rungs of corporate leadership, despite their increasing presence in the workforce. This period also ignited discussions around work-life balance, as many women strived to juggle their burgeoning careers with family responsibilities. Despite these discussions and the strides made, many women still found themselves stalled in middle management, their aspirations of climbing higher unmet.

Now, let's shift our gaze to the here and now. The 21st century has witnessed incredible progress, with women leading the charge. As of 2023, women hold 8.1% of CEO positions—a figure that, while still modest, marks a significant leap from decades past. Furthermore, initiatives promoting diversity and inclusion have become more common place, encouraging organizations to cultivate fairer and more inclusive environments.

Yet, despite these strides, the workspace is still riddled with persistent challenges that hold women back. Sheryl Sandberg once pointed out, *"The glass ceiling may have cracks, but it is not yet shattered."* This metaphor hits close to home today, capturing the complex reality women face in the workplace: celebrated for their successes on one side but quietly hemmed in by barriers on the other.

One such barrier is the notorious "broken rung" at the very first step up to manager. For every 100 men promoted to this first rung, only 87 women make the same ascent, with even fewer women of color joining their ranks. This early bottleneck severely restricts the pool of women eligible for upper management and leadership roles, perpetuating a cycle that's hard to break.

Beyond structural obstacles, women in the workplace often encounter microaggressions—those subtle, often unintentional behaviors that can undercut their professional contributions. Amidst these challenges, the true power of taking charge of our own careers comes sharply into focus. Yes, we need systemic changes to level the playing field, but the influence of personal agency is undeniable. This is about truly understanding your worth and stepping forward with confidence to claim your space.

Think of it like a phoenix rising from the ashes—embodying resilience and renewal. Why do we rise? We rise to lead, to innovate, and to mentor the next generation of women who will stand on our shoulders. By standing up for ourselves—whether negotiating for better pay, pursuing a promotion, or seeking further professional development—we can alter our career paths for the better. Understanding this reality is key to thriving in today's professional world. Yes, it's full of challenges, but there are also plenty of chances for those ready to grab them.

This book is here to stand by your side as you tackle these challenges and soar in your career. Together, we'll dive into twelve powerful strategies that will equip you to take the reins of your professional journey. Each strategy springs from real-life experiences and is tailored to help you walk with confidence. Whether it's about making your voice heard in meetings or building a network that genuinely backs you, each chapter is dedicated to your growth and success.

We'll also explore how to strike that sweet spot between professional achievements and personal happiness. You'll learn how to stand up for yourself, negotiate with finesse, and create environments that uplift the women around you.

As you bring these strategies into play, you'll see yourself thriving, staking your claim and redefining what success looks like for you. Let's embrace this journey together. This is our time to shine, to rise like a phoenix, and lead the way forward.

# CHAPTER 1

# SPEAK UP: FINDING YOUR VOICE AND MAKING IT HEARD

A corporate office comes alive during a crucial team meeting, with professionals from various departments all ready to help with a big project. Among them is a highly competent woman who has been with the company for years. She's armed with innovative ideas and sharp insights, yet as the discussion heats up, she finds herself hesitating. While her male colleagues take turns dominating the conversation, her own ideas linger unspoken. Despite her expertise, she feels overshadowed and struggles to assert herself.

This scenario isn't rare; it's a familiar story in workplaces worldwide. Many women find it challenging to find their voice in professional settings, and this struggle is often compounded by a mix of cultural, societal, and personal barriers.

From a young age, many women are taught to value being polite, accommodating, and to steer clear of confrontation. These societal norms can deeply influence behavior, making it tough for women to assert themselves at work where assertiveness is often mistaken for aggression.

Then there's the fear of repercussions. Speaking up comes with risks-risks of being labeled bossy, aggressive, or difficult. These aren't baseless fears either. Studies have shown that women who assert themselves at work can face more backlash than men in similar positions. This fear can keep even the most capable women quiet.

Confidence, or the lack thereof, also plays a critical role. Many women grapple with imposter syndrome—a nagging feeling of self-doubt and a fear of being exposed as a fraud, despite evident success and capabilities. This lack of confidence can make them second-guess their worth and hesitate to share their valuable perspectives.

The "Women in the Workplace" report by McKinsey & Company highlights another layer to this issue: women are less likely than men to speak up in meetings and are often interrupted or overlooked when they do. Especially in male-dominated industries, the challenge intensifies, with women 1.4 times more likely to feel silenced on matters of bias at work.

Understanding these dynamics is the first step towards change.

## Voice Your Vision: Why Speaking Up Matters

The crucial next step involves breaking through these barriers and discovering one's voice, realizing its powerful influence in reshaping the workplace. Speaking up in the workplace is a key driver of career advancement. When you put your ideas and opinions out there, you're showcasing your expertise and potential to lead. This visibility is vital; it can open doors to recognition, promotions, and broader opportunities.

Beyond climbing the career ladder, finding your voice significantly boosts your ability to influence decisions and drive change within your organization. Your ideas and efforts play a crucial role in guiding projects and crafting strategies that pave the way to success, benefiting you and your company. This level of influence underscores the importance of your input and establishes you as a thought leader in your field.

Moreover, the act of speaking up is intrinsically linked to building confidence. Each time you voice your thoughts and see them acknowledged and valued, your confidence gets a boost. This creates a virtuous cycle where increased confidence fuels further assertiveness, leading to more opportunities for professional growth and fulfillment.

In this way, finding your voice is about making an impact on your career, your workplace, and your personal development.

## Finding My Voice

I understand that talking about finding one's voice and its advantages might sound simple, but I know firsth and that the journey there is anything but easy. So, let me tell you my story. This story starts in my childhood, long before the boardrooms and professional accolades, back when I was a student in a convent school. Taught from a young age to always be polite and respectful, my classmates and I embraced these values deeply, as they were particularly emphasized in our all-girls school environment.

I remember a specific incident that occurred during a school sports day. I was competing in a 100-meter dash. It was a close race, but I crossed the finish line first—or at least I believed I had. The finish was so tight that the student who finished just a fraction of a second after me ran directly to the teacher at the finish line and was declared the winner. Tentatively, I approached the teacher to explain that I had touched the ribbon first. My voice was meek, hesitant; I lacked the confidence to assert myself fully. My teacher dismissed my claim without much consideration.

What stung more than losing the race was the realization that I hadn't found my voice to speak up effectively. I had politely accepted the decision without advocating for myself. This pattern followed me throughout my school years. Whenever I needed to express disagreement or present a challenge, especially to someone in a position of authority like a senior or a teacher, I held back. I believed that being assertive might make me seem rude or demanding, confusing assertiveness with aggression.

As I transitioned into the professional world, that early habit of holding back, of muffling my own voice, unknowingly followed me. In meetings, I would tentatively make a point, but it seemed to vanish into thin air—unheard amid more assertive voices. Politeness became my default; I would let it go, believing it was the respectful thing to do. But this soon turned into a pattern, and staying quiet, especially around senior colleagues, became second nature. The less I spoke, the harder it became to break this cycle. I allowed others to interrupt me, and over time, I found myself fading into silence during meetings entirely.

The real jolt came when I was overlooked for a promotion. The feedback was as clear as it was painful: while my work was exemplary, my lack of assertiveness and my silence in team meetings were seen as shortcomings. I felt like I'd been punched in the gut. That moment was a stark turning point for me.

Reflecting on this, I traced the roots back to my school days. Over the years, I had equated being polite with being silent, with being the person who knows the answer yet speaks too softly, who lets others take the floor, becoming someone polite yet invisible and unheard.

This realization sparked a change in me. Being polite didn't have to mean being quiet. It was time to be assertively polite. I committed to change: I prepared meticulously for every meeting, armed with insights to ensure my contributions were heard and not merely echoed by someone else. If interrupted, I learned to hold my ground politely but firmly, saying, "Actually, I brought up that point first. Let me finish, and then I'd love to hear your thoughts."

Taking those initial steps to assertively take control and speak up at meetings was transformative. It felt like stepping into another life, one where my voice echoed clearly across the room. I couldn't help but wonder, why had I kept myself silent for so many years?

This newfound assertiveness marked a significant shift in my career trajectory, and there was no turning back. Often, I find myself as the only woman in a room full of senior men, but now, I ensure my voice is both heard and felt. Whether it's advocating for increased budgets, kick-starting new initiatives, influencing senior stakeholders, or addressing challenging situations, I stand my ground.

I've learned to speak slowly, clearly, and loudly enough to command everyone's attention before making my points. There's a profound joy in possessing the confidence and self-belief to speak up—it didn't come easy, but through self-reflection and consistent practice, I've made it part of who I am.

Now, I'm eager to pass on what I've learned about cultivating this confidence and self-belief. I'll be drawing from my own experiences as well as the countless interactions I've had with professionals throughout my career.

## Mastering Executive Presence: Confidence, Clarity, and Gravitas

Let's kick things off by exploring the fundamentals of Executive Presence. In today's competitive workplace, the concept of executive presence has become crucial, especially for women aiming to climb the career ladder. Executive presence is often seen as the magic blend of confidence, clarity, and charisma. It's a critical attribute for leaders, but many women face unique challenges in developing and showcasing this presence effectively.

Despite their qualifications and hard work, women are still under represented in senior leadership positions. One of the factors contributing to this disparity is the struggle to exhibit executive presence. This vital trait is frequently misunderstood or undervalued compared to their male counterparts.

Let's talk about some common missteps women make when trying to develop executive presence. Often, there's an over-emphasis on competence. Many women focus intensely on proving their technical skills and expertise, which is important, but can sometimes overshadow other crucial aspects of executive presence like communication and interpersonal skills. This can make it difficult to be seen as a holistic leader.

Another pitfall is underestimating the importance of visibility. Many women shy away from self-promotion, believing their work should speak for itself. While humility is a virtue, in the professional world, being visible is essential. If people don't know about your accomplishments, they might overlook you for leadership opportunities.

Struggling with confidence is another hurdle. Women are more likely to doubt their abilities and hesitate to take on new challenges unless they feel fully prepared. This contrasts with men, who might proceed with less certainty, relying on the confidence that they can figure things out along the way. This hesitation can lead to missed opportunities and slower career advancement.

Understanding these common missteps is a primary step towards mastering executive presence. Next up, it's essential to delve into why it's particularly crucial for women in the workplace.

## Why Executive Presence Matters for Women

First and foremost, a strong executive presence enables women to command respect. It's about walking into a room and immediately being taken seriously by everyone around the table—peers and superiors alike. When you project confidence and composure, people listen more intently, and your ideas receive the consideration they deserve.

Moreover, executive presence extends beyond personal impact; it significantly enhances your ability to influence decisions. With this trait finely honed, you can steer discussions and have a substantial say in the direction your team, department, or even the entire organization takes.

Lastly, executive presence is integral in building trust and credibility. Effective leadership stands on the pillars of confidence and capability. When the people you work with view you as a leader possessing these qualities, it naturally builds a foundation of trust. This trust opens doors to more leadership opportunities and amplifies your influence within the organization.

## The Confidence Blueprint - Building a Stronger You

Let's begin by unpacking one of the most crucial elements of executive presence: **confidence**. Today's professional women are often well-educated and bring a rich diversity of skills and perspectives to the table. Yet, they frequently find themselves in environments where their contributions are overlooked or undervalued. This is particularly noticeable in meetings where, too often, men dominate the conversation and decision-making processes.

Janice Tomich, an expert in communication and leadership, notes that women may hold back in meetings due to fears of being interrupted or having their ideas co-opted by male colleagues. This ongoing struggle undermines a woman's confidence and her ability to assert her executive presence.

## The Confidence Hurdles

Several factors contribute to this confidence gap in the workplace:

> ***Fear of Rejection or Criticism:*** Many women hesitate to express their opinions or aspire to leadership roles because they fear negative feedback or rejection. This can be traced back to experiences where their contributions were not appropriately acknowledged or valued.

***Perfectionism:*** There's often a pressure for women to feel fully prepared and flawless before they feel comfortable taking on new challenges. This quest for perfection can be paralyzing, preventing them from seizing opportunities that could boost their visibility and self-assurance.

***Internalizing Biases:*** Societal and workplace biases that subtly suggest women are less competent or authoritative than men can deeply affect self-esteem. When these biases are internalized, they significantly hinder a woman's willingness to step forward and lead.

## Unlocking Confidence: The Key to Thriving in the Workplace

Confidence is a professional tool that empowers women to command respect and influence decisions. When a woman projects confidence, her ideas and opinions resonate more strongly, ensuring they are taken seriously by peers and superiors alike. This level of respect enhances her visibility and builds trust, establishing her as a reliable leader within her field. Moreover, confidence enables active participation in decision-making processes, ensuring that a woman's unique perspectives contribute to more balanced and effective outcomes. It also arms her against the biases that might otherwise undermine her efforts, allowing her to demonstrate her true capability and leadership potential.

Despite the clear benefits, building confidence can be a challenge, especially when traditional workplace dynamics often do not favor outspokenness in women. Many women believe that accumulating experience is enough to naturally boost confidence, but this isn't always the case. Waiting until one feels fully prepared can actually reinforce doubts and lead to missed opportunities.

Instead, adopting a proactive approach to preparation can make all the difference. Actively preparing for specific situations, like rehearsing key points for a presentation or anticipating questions for a meeting, can solidify knowledge and boost confidence.

Moreover, embracing a mindset of experimentation—stepping into new roles, trying out new ideas, and even making mistakes—can be incredibly beneficial. This approach encourages learning from both successes and failures, gradually building genuine self-assurance that extends beyond mere familiarity with tasks.

Assertive communication is another crucial skill, one that many women struggle with for fear of being seen as aggressive or unlikable. I've previously shared how I faced and overcame this fear. To navigate this fear, women can enhance their communication by being clear and direct. This involves practicing assertive communication techniques such as maintaining eye contact, using a firm tone, and cutting out filler words. Phrases like "I'm not finished talking" or "What I'm saying is important" can be instrumental in reclaiming the floor when interrupted.

Setting boundaries in conversations is also key. It might involve politely but firmly addressing interruptions and insisting on finishing points before others speak. Role-playing with trusted colleagues or mentors can also be incredibly effective. It provides a safe space to practice and refine assertive communication, helping women feel more prepared and confident in real-life scenarios.

Another common challenge is the tendency among women to tackle workplace hurdles alone, which can be isolating and undermine their confidence. Women might also hesitate to seek support due to fears of appearing weak or dependent.

To counter this, actively building a support network is essential. This network should include supportive colleagues, mentors and allies who recognize and advocate for one's professional growth. Moreover, seeking mentorship from experienced professionals can provide invaluable guidance.

Another key factor is positive self-talk. Many professionals, particularly women, struggle with negative self-talk and self-doubt, often as a result of internalizing societal biases and undervaluing their own accomplishments. This leads to imposter syndrome, where despite evident success, a person feels undeserving and doubts their abilities.

I've seen many capable women in the workplace who struggle with their self-worth. For example, a colleague once confided that she felt overshadowed by her male peers and supervisors, who seemed to question her contributions. Despite consistently receiving praise for her work, she began to seek external validation, which only intensified her self-doubt. This constant search for approval made her question her own competence, causing her confidence to wane.

To combat these undermining thoughts, adopting positive affirmations is a powerful tool. Simple yet effective, positive affirmations involve reminding yourself of your strengths and past successes. For example, starting the day by affirming, "I am competent, skilled, and bring valuable ideas to the table," can set a positive tone and enhance self-assurance.

By actively engaging in these strategies, you can shift from a cycle of self-doubt to one of self-empowerment and confidence. This confidence is essential for commanding respect, influencing decisions and challenging the biases that often hold women back.

## Crystal Clear: The Power of Clarity in Executive Presence

Clarity is the next essential ingredient in the recipe for effective executive presence. It's about the ability to convey ideas succinctly and powerfully, ensuring that your messages resonate with your audience. Yet, achieving this clarity can sometimes be a taller order for women, impacting their ability to make a mark and expand their influence.

## The Clarity Challenge

Today, women in the workplace bring a wealth of valuable perspectives. Despite this, many find that their communications sometimes lack the clarity that stamps authority and commands respect. This often stems from several challenges:

> ***Over-Explaining:*** There's a tendency among women to feel they must provide exhaustive details to substantiate their points. This over-explanation can water down the core message, making it less impactful and more cumbersome to grasp.

***Hesitation and Self-Doubt:*** Doubts about whether their ideas are worthwhile can lead women to hold back or communicate in ways that seem uncertain. This hesitation can cloud their messages, making them appear less confident and assertive.

***Being Overlooked or Interrupted:*** It's not uncommon for women to be interrupted in meetings or to have their ideas hijacked by others, often male colleagues. This disruptive pattern can significantly hinder their ability to deliver clear and assertive messages.

## Why Clarity Matters

For women aiming to thrive in the corporate world and cement their executive presence, mastering clarity in communication is non-negotiable. It's pivotal for several reasons:

***Ensuring Your Voice is Heard:*** Clear communication cuts through the noise, ensuring your ideas are both heard and understood. This is crucial for influencing decisions and driving meaningful change within an organization.

***Establishing Authority:*** When you communicate with clarity, you position yourself as an authority in your field. This clear, confident expression helps you garner respect and opens doors to higher leadership roles.

***Building Trust:*** Being clear and concise in your communications fosters trust and transparency—two pillars essential for effective leadership and teamwork.

## Enhancing Clarity: Strategic Communication for Impact

Let's explore practical strategies to sharpen your communication skills and ensure your messages hit the mark every time.

A common pitfall for many professional women is providing too much context or detail in their explanations. To counter this, adopting the Pyramid Principle can be transformative. This method involves leading with your main point and then layering on supporting details as needed. Such a structure ensures that your core message is front and center, easily understandable from the get-go.

Another effective tool is organizing your thoughts into bullet points before speaking. This technique aids in delivering your message in a clear, structured format that's easy for your audience to follow and remember. It helps keep your communications concise and focused, preventing unnecessary diversions.

While verbal communication is powerful, complementing it with visual aids can significantly enhance understanding and engagement. Incorporating slide decks is one strategic approach. A well-designed slide deck that highlights key points and includes impactful visuals can make your presentations more engaging and clearer. Visual aids can simplify complex ideas and emphasize crucial points, making your message more memorable.

Additionally, using charts and diagrams can be particularly effective in meetings or reports where data needs to be conveyed. These tools offer a clear visual representation of relationships and data, making abstract concepts more concrete and understandable. By integrating these visual elements, you can enhance the clarity and impact of your communications, ensuring your ideas are fully grasped and appreciated.

## Commanding the Room: The Power of Gravitas

Gravitas is a key element of executive presence, particularly for women aiming to stand out in the workplace. It's that air of seriousness and dignity that naturally commands respect and attention. Yet, many women face unique challenges in cultivating gravitas, which can impede their professional growth and influence.

## Understanding the Challenges to Gravitas

Despite the high competence women bring to the workplace, their ability to project gravitas is often compromised by several behavioral patterns. For instance, the tendency to over-apologize, even when unnecessary, can significantly undermine their authority. Such apologies, though often well-intentioned as a form of politeness, might send a signal of uncertainty or weakness.

Moreover, many women habitually use qualifiers like "I think" or "maybe" in their communication. While intended to soften statements, these qualifiers can unfortunately make their assertions appear less confident and undermine their decisiveness. Additionally, the reluctance to engage in confrontations or tough conversations can further diminish a woman's perceived leadership qualities, as it may be misconstrued as a lack of backbone or clarity in decision-making.

## Why Gravitas Matters

The importance of gravitas in the workplace cannot be overstated. Gravitas enables women to command the respect necessary to make their voices heard and their contributions taken seriously.

Furthermore, gravitas is a hallmark of strong leadership. It helps women establish themselves as credible, respected leaders who are not just part of the conversation but are guiding it. This presence is essential in handling both daily tasks and in critical moments that demand firm leadership and clear direction.

## Empowering Your Voice: Practical Strategies to Cultivate Gravitas

For women aiming to enhance their gravitas, I would like to offer a few strategies that transform challenges into strengths.

A common issue is that women often inadvertently undermine their own authority by over-apologizing or peppering their speech with qualifiers. To shift away from this habit, it's crucial to adopt more assertive language. For instance, rather than saying, "I think we should consider this option," it's more impactful to state, "We should consider this option." This simple change in phrasing can significantly enhance the authority of your statements.

Another area where women can strengthen their gravitas is in their approach to confrontation. The tendency to shy away from difficult conversations for fear of being seen as aggressive can actually signal a lack of decisiveness. Preparing for these conversations is key—anticipate potential challenges and rehearse your responses. Techniques such as deep breathing, taking a moment to pause before responding, and maintaining a steady tone can help you stay composed and convey a sense of control and authority.

Often, self-doubt or a lower profile within an organization can prevent women from being seen as potential leaders. To counter this, actively seeking visibility is crucial. Engage more in meetings, volunteer for projects that are highly visible, and connect with influential figures within your organization. Additionally, investing in your professional development through leadership training or public speaking courses can provide you with the skills necessary to stand out. These efforts improve your own self-perception and how others perceive you, paving the way for leadership opportunities.

## The Power of Words: Shaping Perceptions and Outcomes

We've talked about the significance of executive presence for women professionals. Now, let's zoom into another equally significant aspect: finding and using your voice effectively in the workplace. This brings us to the incredible power of language. Nelson Mandela once said, "It is never my custom to use words lightly." His words remind us that language is a potent tool that shapes perceptions and outcomes. Language doesn't just convey information; it molds our professional image and influences our career trajectories.

Speaking with confidence and assertiveness positions you as a leader and a credible authority in your field. Using language that conveys certainty and conviction can make a significant difference in how your contributions are received.

For instance, instead of cushioning your suggestions with qualifiers, direct statements like, "I recommend this approach because it aligns with our objectives," can assert your expertise and insight more effectively.

Moreover, clear and impactful language enhances your ability to sway decisions. When you articulate your thoughts clearly and persuasively, you're more likely to drive meaningful changes and steer critical discussions. This ability is particularly important in high-stake meetings where strategic decisions are made. Furthermore, the choice of words can dramatically shape your professional image. Opting for language that exudes professionalism and respect helps in building a persona that commands trust and admiration from both colleagues and superiors.

## Strategies to Own Your Voice

We've discussed the impact of language on professional presence, and now it's time to dive into actionable strategies that can help you harness the power of words to assert yourself and thrive in the workplace.

One common challenge among us is the tendency to use language that diminishes authority. To counter this, practice eliminating unnecessary apologies from your speech. Instead of saying, "I'm sorry, but I have a question," you can confidently say, "I have a question." This small shift removes the unnecessary apology and presents you as more assertive.

Another area where women often struggle is in presenting their ideas. Prefacing suggestions with tentative language or self-deprecating remarks can make you seem unsure of your contributions. This behavior often stems from internalized self-doubt or fear of being perceived as overly aggressive. To overcome this, practice speaking with confidence. Instead of saying, "This might be a whimsical idea, but...," try "I propose this approach..." This approach shows that you believe in the value of your ideas.

Additionally, indirect language can lead to misunderstandings and can make you seem indecisive. Women often beat around the bush when making requests or giving feedback. To address this, practice being direct and clear. Instead of saying, "It would be great if someone could handle this task," say, "Please handle this task." This direct approach leaves no room for ambiguity and shows decisiveness.

When giving feedback, specificity is key. Instead of vague suggestions like "You might want to consider doing this differently," use direct language: "I recommend you do this differently." This makes your feedback clearer amd reinforces your leadership.

These changes, though small, can have a profound impact on your professional image and career advancement.

## Power Speak: Words and Phrases That Project Authority and Initiative

It's equally important to focus on specific language that can further establish your leadership presence. Here, I present a curated list of words and phrases that effectively convey authority and initiative—essential tools for any woman looking to strengthen her position in the workplace.

## Words and Phrases That Convey Authority

1. ***"I Recommend…"***

   - *Context:* When suggesting a course of action or a solution.

   - *Example:* Replace "I think we should consider this option" with "I recommend we pursue this option because it aligns with our strategic goals."

2. ***"I'm Confident That…"***

   - *Context:* When expressing certainty about an idea or decision.

   - *Example:* Change "I believe this might work" to "I'm confident that this approach will yield positive results based on our previous data."

3. ***"My Analysis Shows…"***

   - *Context:* When presenting data or findings.

   - *Example:* Instead of "I think the data suggests," use "My analysis shows that our customer retention rates have improved by 15%."

4. ***"I Propose…"***

   - *Context:* When introducing a new idea or plan.

   - *Example:* Shift from "Maybe we could try" to "I propose we implement a new marketing strategy to target younger demographics."

5. ***"I'm Certain…"***

   - *Context:* When expressing strong conviction.

- *Example:* Instead of the tentative "I'm not sure, but I think," opt for "I'm certain that this project will meet our deadlines."

To truly stand out and lead effectively in the workplace, it's essential to use language that also demonstrates initiative. Here are some powerful phrases that can help you take charge and drive action in your professional environment.

## Words and Phrases That Convey Initiative

1. ***"I Will Take Charge Of..."***

- *Context:* When volunteering for a task or project.

- *Example:* Instead of saying, "I can help with this," assert, "I will take charge of coordinating the team for this project."

2. ***"Let's Move Forward With..."***

- *Context:* When driving action and decision-making.

- *Example:* Replace "Should we start this?" with "Let's move forward with the implementation of the new software."

3. ***"I Have Identified..."***

- *Context:* When highlighting problems or opportunities.

- *Example:* Instead of saying, "There might be an issue," state, "I have identified a potential issue with our supply chain that needs addressing."

4. ***"I'm Taking the Initiative To..."***

- *Context:* When proactively addressing a need or opportunity.

- *Example:* Instead of "I think we should look into," use "I'm taking the initiative to research new vendors for our upcoming project."

5. **"I Commit To…"**

- *Context:* When making a commitment.

- *Example:* Swap "I'll try to" with "I commit to delivering the report by the end of the week.

Let's take a glimpse into how the powerful words we've discussed translate into action with a couple of real-world scenarios. These examples will show you how small changes in language can significantly impact your professional presence and effectiveness.

## Scenario 1: Leading a Team Meeting

Think about being a manager who's running a team meeting to talk about a new project. Your goal is to assert your authority and guide your team toward a decisive action plan. Instead of saying, "I think we should consider using a new project management tool. Maybe it will help us stay organized," you could say, "I recommend we adopt a new project management tool to enhance our organization and efficiency." This shift in language clearly demonstrates your confidence and decisiveness, making your suggestion more compelling.

## Scenario 2: Presenting a Proposal

Now, picture yourself as an executive presenting a proposal to senior leadership. You need to convey confidence and initiative to gain approval for your strategy. Rather than saying, "I believe this might work, but I'm not sure. We could try implementing this strategy," you would say, "I'm confident that this strategy will work based on our market analysis. I propose we implement it in the next quarter." This adjustment projects assurance and positions you as a proactive leader who is ready to take decisive action.

## Beyond Words: Mastering the Art of Non-Verbal Communication

Having explored the impact of strategic language use, let's turn our attention to another vital aspect of communication—non-verbal cues. In the modern workplace, your body language and tone of voice are just as crucial as the words you choose. For women professionals aiming to reinforce their authority, confidence, and initiative, mastering these non-verbal aspects is essential.

## Non-Verbal Communication in the Workplace

- **Closed Body Language:** Many women may unconsciously adopt closed body language, such as crossed arms or a slouched posture. These gestures can convey insecurity or defensiveness, contradicting messages meant to project confidence and authority.

- **Hesitant Tone:** Using a hesitant or high-pitched tone can also undermine the speaker's authority, making her seem unsure or less convincing, regardless of the expertise she brings to the table.

- **Lack of Eye Contact:** Avoiding eye contact is another significant barrier. It can signal a lack of confidence and engagement, making it harder for the message to resonate with the audience and reducing the speaker's perceived credibility.

## The Power of Body Language and Tone

The effective use of body language and tone is critical for women to fully thrive in their careers. These non-verbal cues play a key role in how women are perceived in professional settings:

- **Projecting Confidence:** Adopting open and assertive body language, along with a firm and steady tone, can dramatically enhance perceptions of self-assurance and credibility.

- **Enhancing Authority:** Strong non-verbal cues can significantly enhance verbal messages. When your body language aligns with your words, it reinforces your role as an authoritative figure, making your statements more compelling.

- **Engaging and Influencing:** Effective non-verbal communication captures and holds the audience's attention, making interactions more engaging and persuasive. When you speak with confidence and maintain appropriate eye contact, your audience is more likely to listen and be influenced by your ideas.

## Mastering Body Language and Tone

To fully harness the power of non-verbal communication, we can adopt several strategies that reinforce our messages and project authority. Let's explore how body language and tone can be used to enhance professional presence.

Practicing power poses can be highly effective. For example, standing with your feet shoulder-width apart and hands on your hips can boost your confidence and project authority. Research by Amy Cuddy suggests that these poses can increase feelings of confidence and reduce stress.

In addition to power poses, using open gestures like uncrossed arms and open palms can convey openness and approachability. These gestures make you appear more confident and engaged, enhancing the overall impact of your communication.

Another common issue is using a hesitant or high-pitched tone, which can undermine authority and make you seem unsure. This often stems from nervousness or a desire to be perceived as polite. To address this, practice speaking in a lower pitch, which naturally conveys authority and confidence. Recording yourself and adjusting your pitch can help you find a tone that sounds both assertive and natural.

Speaking at a controlled pace is also crucial. Instead of rushing through your words, maintain a steady pace, and strategically pause to emphasize key points. This approach not only enhances clarity but also allows your audience to absorb and reflect on your message.

Avoiding eye contact can signal a lack of confidence and engagement. To combat this, practice sustained eye contact with your audience. Start by making eye contact with individuals for a few seconds before moving on to the next person. This practice can help you convey confidence and engagement.

Using eye contact to engage different parts of the audience can make your presentation more dynamic and interactive. It shows that you are connected with your audience and invested in their response to your message.

These adjustments in body language and tone are about transforming how you communicate to ensure your messages are delivered with confidence and authority.

## Practical Mastery

Having explored the enhancement of body language, tone, and language use, let's explore practical exercises to help you discover your voice, express yourself confidently, and ensure you are heard.

## Exercise 1: Tone Adjustment

Developing a confident and controlled tone is crucial. Start by recording yourself reading a passage aloud. Listen to the playback and pay attention to your pitch and pace. Practice speaking with a lower pitch and at a controlled pace. Record yourself again and compare the two recordings. Notice the differences and continue practicing until your tone sounds assertive and natural.

## Exercise 2: Eye Contact Drill

Maintaining confident and engaging eye contact can transform your interactions. Practice this by making eye contact with a partner or even in front of a mirror. Hold the eye contact for a few seconds before shifting to another point. Gradually increase the duration of your eye contact to build comfort and confidence. This exercise helps you connect better with your audience, making your communication more impactful.

## Exercise 3: Open Gestures

Using open and assertive body language enhances your overall presence. Practice speaking with open gestures, such as keeping your arms uncrossed and your palms open. You can record yourself or ask for feedback from a colleague to ensure your gestures appear natural and confident. This practice helps in making your communication more approachable and engaging.

As you integrate these exercises into your routine, you'll find yourself becoming more comfortable and confident in speaking up. In your next meeting or presentation, make a conscious effort to speak up. Share your ideas, ask questions, and contribute to the discussion. Remember, your voice is valuable and deserves to be heard. Use this opportunity to practice assertive language, maintain confident body language, and engage fully with your audience.

Your journey to finding your voice begins with a single step. Make it count.

# CHAPTER 2

# EMOTIONAL SMARTS: HARNESSING EMOTIONAL INTELLIGENCE AT WORK

From a young age, many of us have been surrounded by phrases like "women are too emotional" or "women are naturally more empathetic." How many times have you heard these phrases tossed around? If you're like me, it's probably more often than you'd care to count. These common sayings, while seemingly benign, can actually set a powerful backdrop for both constraining and empowering beliefs. The stereotype that women are more emotional than men is particularly pervasive and can influence how female leaders are viewed and evaluated, ultimately impacting their career trajectories and dynamics within the workplace.

Beyond their broader impact, these stereotypes seep into our personal self-view, shaping how we perceive our own capabilities and roles. The internalization of such beliefs can lead to self-doubt and a pressured feeling that we must continually prove our competence, especially in environments traditionally dominated by men.

However, it's not just about challenging these stereotypes; it's about rewriting them. Developing emotional intelligence emerges as a potent tool in this rewrite, empowering women to master their professional environments with greater finesse. When we get a grip on our emotions and manage them wisely, what seems like a weakness can actually become our biggest strength. It's all about ensuring our empathetic abilities to improve how we communicate, lead, and bounce back from challenges at work.

## Emotional Intelligence at Play: Navigating Workplace Challenges

Consider how emotional intelligence, or a lack of it, can significantly sway workplace outcomes. By diving into examples, we can grasp the deep impact emotional intelligence has in professional environments, highlighting the challenges and framing the context for its profound influence.

I want to share a story about a talented professional named Natasha. She recently joined a traditional firm in a male-dominated core business function. From the start, she faced constant challenges to her authority, particularly from an old-timer on the team. This individual, who had long aspired to her position, saw her as an outsider and a threat.

During team meetings, this colleague would frequently undercut her by questioning her decisions and strategies. These confrontations were both personal and public, eroding her authority in front of the entire team. The situation reached a tipping point one day when, after a series of such challenges, Natasha felt her frustration boiling over. Despite her usual composure, the continuous undermining pushed her to react emotionally. In a moment of intense pressure, she raised her voice and responded more sharply than intended.

This outburst, rare for Natasha, shocked her team and unfortunately gave her detractor more ammunition to question her suitability for the leadership role. Later, reflecting on this incident, Natasha found herself wrestling with self-doubt. She questioned her leadership abilities and feared that her emotional reaction had confirmed the stereotype of women being too emotional for leadership roles. This incident made her deeply introspective about her approach to leadership and the balance between being assertive and maintaining professional composure in challenging situations.

In the days that followed, Natasha realized the importance of regaining her team's respect and authority. Reflecting on the incident, she recognized that her reaction wasn't a failure of her leadership capabilities, but rather a gap in applying emotional intelligence in the heat of the moment. She began seeking strategies to handle such confrontations more effectively, focusing on maintaining her calm and using measured responses to disarm and diffuse challenging situations. Integrating emotional intelligence into her leadership, Natasha earned to anticipate potential conflicts and understand the underlying issues driving confrontational behavior. This approach allowed her to address concerns proactively and empathetically, preventing escalations and gradually diminishing the bias against her. Her journey became one of learning to reshape a challenging workplace dynamic, striving to lead and transform the culture of her team into one of respect and mutual support.

## Peeling Back the Layers of Emotional Intelligence

The experiences of Natasha underline just how transformative emotional intelligence (EI) can be in the professional lives of women. This insight brings us deeper into the concept of emotional intelligence, often referred to as EQ. It's a fundamental element in nurturing relationships, thriving at work, and improving all areas of life.Through EQ, professionals like Natasha tackle complex workplace dynamics with poise and effectiveness, showcasing that emotional acumen is integral to personal and career success.

Daniel Goleman, who popularized the concept in his 1995 book *Emotional Intelligence*, describes EI as the ability to perceive, understand, manage, and regulate emotions both in ourselves and in others. He identifies critical components such as self-awareness, self-regulation, motivation, empathy, and social skills, each playing a vital role in shaping how effectively individuals interact with their colleagues and navigate workplace dynamics.

Women in the workplace often encounter unique challenges that can influence their career trajectory and overall job satisfaction. For instance, women are frequently expected to undertake more emotional labor, such as providing emotional support to colleagues. This crucial contribution often goes unrecognized and unrewarded, potentially leading to emotional exhaustion and decreased job satisfaction. Moreover, to be perceived as effective leaders, women are often pressured to adopt traditional masculine traits, a demand that can lead to emotional burnout and stress.

In male-dominated environments, women may feel the need to suppress their emotions to fit in or be taken seriously, which can lead to increased stress. Without a clear understanding of their own emotional triggers, women might struggle with effective communication and decision-making.

Difficulty in managing emotions can result in impulsive responses that may harm professional relationships and undermine a woman's authority and credibility. Neglecting to understand or respond to the emotions of colleagues can erode trust and hinder the formation of cooperative and supportive team dynamics. Limited social skills can be a barrier to effective networking and career advancement, as forming professional relationships is key to opening doors and creating opportunities in any career field.

Grasping these dynamics is key to unlocking the full potential of emotional intelligence. Now, let's delve into why emotional intelligence is crucial for women in the workplace.

Women with high emotional intelligence bring clarity and depth to workplace communications. They articulate their thoughts and feelings clearly, reducing misunderstandings and nurturing an atmosphere of open and honest dialogue. This ability to communicate effectively is complemented by their skill in active listening—fully concentrating, understanding, and thoughtfully responding to colleagues. Such capabilities make them invaluable team members, adept at mediating conflicts and facilitating collaborative efforts.

Moreover, women often have a natural proficiency in reading non-verbal cues such as body language and facial expressions, a key component of emotional intelligence. This skill allows for more nuanced communication and a deeper understanding of team dynamics, which is particularly useful in leadership roles where non-verbal cues can provide critical information about team morale and individual well-being.

When conflicts arise, as they inevitably do in any dynamic work environment, women equipped with high EI are better prepared to handle them constructively. They approach disputes with empathy and understanding, inspiring a cooperative rather than confrontational atmosphere, which is essential for long-term team cohesion.

Furthermore, emotional intelligence is instrumental in building trust and rapport. Women who exhibit high EI are seen as more relatable and trustworthy, qualities that lay the foundation for strong professional relationships and a supportive work culture. This trust is crucial for creating an environment where ideas can be exchanged freely and innovation can flourish.

Lastly, the impact of emotional intelligence extends to enhancing team dynamics. Women with strong EI are sensitive to the emotional needs and undercurrents within their teams. By addressing these effectively, they help maintain high morale and satisfaction, which translates into better overall performance and job fulfillment.

Emotional intelligence, therefore, is a profound influence that women can leverage to reshape their workplaces into more collaborative, understanding, and productive environments.

## Cultivating Self-Awareness: The Heart of Emotional Intelligence

Understanding the role of emotional intelligence for women in the workplace reveals its significant benefits, prompting a closer look at its key elements, starting with self-awareness. Self-awareness is at the heart of emotional intelligence, playing a crucial role in both personal and professional development. Self-awareness is about understanding your emotions, thoughts, values, and how they impact your behavior. This crucial skill has two dimensions: internal self-awareness, which focuses on introspection and understanding your own emotions, and external self-awareness, which concerns how others perceive you.

In my experience, I've observed that many women at the workplace are intensely focused on meeting external expectations and proving their competence. This often comes at the expense of acknowledging their internal emotional states. This oversight can create a dissonance between their actions and their true feelings, leading to increased stress and dissatisfaction. It's essential to balance external achievements with internal awareness to maintain overall well-being and job satisfaction.

Do you remember Natasha's story from earlier in our discussion? Reflecting on her experience, it's clear how vital it is to recognize and understand one's emotional triggers. In her case, harsh feedback in a public setting triggered a significant emotional response. As she learned to identify these triggers, she could strategically manage her reactions. This self-awareness allowed her to take deliberate steps to mitigate stress and ensure her decisions were thoughtful and balanced, rather than reactionary. Such insights are invaluable, enabling more calculated and effective responses in challenging workplace dynamics.

This self-knowledge enhances decision-making and improves interactions within a team. For example, a team leader aware of her stress as deadlines approach can proactively adjust project timelines or request additional support, maintaining team morale and productivity.

Studies also emphasize how crucial self-awareness is for achieving success in one's career. HBR identifies self-awareness as a foundational skill for the 21st century. Individuals who understand themselves and how others perceive them are typically more effective, confident, and respected, making them more promotable. This level of self-awareness enables them to navigate professional environments with greater agility, strengthening their capabilities and enhancing their career prospects.

## Mastering Self-Regulation: A Key to Professional Resilience

Let's think back to Natasha's story. We saw how learning to manage her emotions became a turning point in her career. In those moments of intense pressure, where stress threatened to take over, she found that self-regulation was essential. I've noticed that many of us, especially women, often face similar challenges—juggling high expectations, balancing multiple roles, and trying to keep it all together. It's not easy. When stress builds up, it's so easy to react emotionally or make quick decisions that we might later regret. But like Natasha learned, the ability to pause, take a breath, and respond thoughtfully can make all the difference. It's about staying grounded and tackling those tough situations with grace and professionalism, even when everything around you feels chaotic.

The ability to manage stress through self-regulation is crucial for maintaining mental well-being and approaching challenges with resilience. I've learned that those who excel in self-regulation can stay composed under pressure, making them invaluable in handling complex workplace dynamics. I've seen this firsthand—both in my own journey and in observing senior women leaders who handle high-stress situations with remarkable effectiveness.

For me, working on self-regulation has been a long process. It's taken years of practice, and I'll admit, I still falter at times. But the difference now is that I know how to bounce back. I've seen how powerful it can be to take that pause, to breathe, and then respond with intention rather than reacting impulsively. It's these moments that have made a real impact, both in my career and in the careers of the women I've admired.

Self-regulation also makes a huge difference when it comes to resolving conflicts. Approaching a disagreement with calm and constructive intent can transform a tense situation into an opportunity for teamwork and collaboration. I've witnessed how staying composed in heated moments can de-escalate tensions and create a more supportive and cooperative environment.

On top of that, self-regulation is key to maintaining professionalism. Keeping your emotions in check, especially when things get stressful, shows that you're reliable and level-headed—qualities that are highly valued in any workplace.

Reflecting on my own experiences, I recall a particularly challenging moment early in my career that underscores the profound impact of self-regulation. I was still finding my footing in the corporate world, eager to impress and make an impact. During a routine team meeting, I was caught off guard when asked to present a project I was not fully prepared for. The feedback from my manager was unexpectedly severe—delivered methodically and without restraint. His critique was sharp, detailed, and public, highlighting every shortfall in my preparation. Surrounded by my peers, I felt each word like a weight, diminishing my confidence by the second.

The humiliation was intense. I struggled to contain my emotions, and tears began to blur my vision. Overwhelmed and embarrassed, I excused myself from the meeting, my mind racing with thoughts of resignation.

In the aftermath of that bruising encounter, I found myself retreating into a shell of avoidance and self-justification. The days that followed were marred by a silent protest—I communicated with my supervisor only through emails, steering clear of any direct interaction. This avoidance did little to resolve the hurt; instead, it only deepened my disengagement from my work. I dragged myself to the office, my enthusiasm dampened by unresolved emotions.

Fast forward a decade, and I found myself in a reminiscent situation—facing harsh criticism in a room full of colleagues. This time, the critique came from a senior leader, and once again, I felt unsupported by my manager, left in the choppy waters of criticism alone. However, the years had equipped me with a crucial tool: the ability to maintain composure. I focused not on the tone or the harsh words but on the substance of the feedback. I took a moment to process, then methodically acknowledged the points raised, clarifying misunderstandings calmly and asserting where I believed there was misinterpretation.

This experience highlighted the profound lessons from my earlier years. Reacting in the heat of the moment—letting emotions control your responses—often leads to negative outcomes. It was not about suppressing emotions but about understanding and channeling them constructively. The key was in the pause: a brief moment to step back, self-regulate, and respond thoughtfully, avoiding the pitfalls of an Amygdala hijack.

## Fueling the Fire Within: The Role of Motivation in Emotional Intelligence

To keep the flame of excellence alive with emotional intelligence, motivation is key. Motivation isn't about ticking boxes or climbing the career ladder for external accolades; it's about an intrinsic drive that fuels personal satisfaction and continuous self-improvement. This form of motivation is rooted deeply in a passion for one's work and a commitment to personal and professional goals.

In my experience as a coach, I've had countless conversations with women who face unique hurdles at work that can drain their intrinsic motivation. Many of them share how persistent gender biases and systemic barriers, like the infamous "glass ceiling" and the "broken rung" phenomenon, often make the professional environment feel less rewarding. These challenges leave them feeling undervalued and overlooked, which inevitably stifles their motivation and hampers their productivity.

Amidst these obstacles, I've observed that women early in their careers might lean heavily on external validation. This reliance can be problematic, particularly in environments where recognition is scarce and gender biases are prevalent. Without external affirmation, motivation can wane, leading to disengagement and a lack of fulfillment.

Furthermore, clarity of professional goals is often another missing piece in the puzzle. In my conversations with young women professionals, I've noticed a trend: many aim too low. To shift this mindset, I encourage them to pursue BHAGs—Big Hairy Ambitious Goals. This concept, coined by Jim Collins and Jerry Porras in their book *Built to Last*, challenges leaders to define visionary goals that are more strategic and emotionally compelling. BHAGs are about dreaming big in a way that ignites sustained passion and commitment.

For women, especially in male-dominated fields, embracing BHAGs can be transformative. It pushes boundaries, challenges the status quo, and inspires a mindset of maximizing potential rather than settling for the minimum. Clear, ambitious goals can provide the motivation needed to excel in challenging environments, making each achievement a stepping stone to greater success.

Addressing these pitfalls is essential because motivation—particularly intrinsic motivation—is a powerhouse for professional advancement. It propels persistence and effort, fuels resilience, and enhances productivity. Motivated women are more likely to set ambitious goals, bounce back from setbacks, and achieve significant career milestones.

Reflecting a broader trend, the Women in the Workplace 2023 report by McKinsey underscores a rising ambition among women: 80% express a desire to advance to the next level, up from 70% in 2019. This shift signals a strong intrinsic motivation among women to climb higher in their careers, despite the obstacles.

## The Art of Empathy: Striking the Right Balance

Alfred Adler beautifully captured the essence of empathy when he said, "Empathy is seeing with the eyes of another, listening with the ears of another, and feeling with the heart of another." Empathy, celebrated for its capacity to comprehend and share the emotions of others, plays a vital role in cultivating strong interpersonal connections and nurturing a supportive workplace culture. It serves as a foundational element for leaders who seek to build unified and motivated teams.

Empathy is often seen as a natural trait for women, perceived to enhance their leadership by enabling them to connect with their teams on a deeper level. However, the challenge often lies in balancing empathy with the necessary assertiveness that leadership demands. Over-empathizing, for instance, can lead women to shoulder the emotional burdens of others, which might lead to stress and eventual burnout. Conversely, under-empathizing—or the failure to adequately perceive and react to the emotions of colleagues—can erode trust and diminish team cooperation.

Recognizing and avoiding these extremes is crucial because empathy profoundly influences workplace dynamics. It builds trust and rapport, which are foundational to effective teamwork. Trust inspires a climate where ideas flow freely, and challenges are met collaboratively, rather than competitively.

I've always been inspired by empathetic leaders who truly understand and address the needs and concerns of their team members. Their knack for tuning into others' emotional wavelengths ensures a compassionate and fair approach to resolving conflicts, proving essential for maintaining a harmonious work environment.

I once had a team member who was juggling multiple challenges at home. Drawing inspiration from empathetic leaders I'd observed before, I arranged a private, supportive meeting to better understand her situation and offer the flexibility she needed. This approach helped her handle her difficulties and enabled her to bounce back stronger. Over time, she rose to become one of our team's top performers, proving just how powerful empathy and supportive leadership can be.

## The Impact of Social Skills in the Professional Arena

Finally, an essential piece of the emotional intelligence puzzle is having strong social skills. This component is centered around the adeptness to interact effectively with others—be it through effective communication, adept conflict management, or the nurturing of strong relationships. These skills are essential for ensuring effective teamwork and leadership.

Observing the challenges women face in the workplace, it's notable that a passive communication style often adopted to avoid conflict can lead to grave misunderstandings and the loss of critical opportunities. This approach might seem to keep the peace, yet it stunts professional growth and the development of meaningful connections that could propel one's career forward.

Social skills extend beyond mere interaction; they are vital for successful collaboration. Individuals who excel in social skills adeptly tackle team dynamics, ensuring a workplace that is productive and positively engaged. These skills empower professionals to be recognized and often fast-tracked for promotions due to their evident contribution to team cohesion and project success.

One of the professionals I coached truly embraced the importance of social skills and saw incredible success as a result. She made it a point to attend professional conferences that aligned with her career goals, both to gain knowledge and to expand her network. During these events, she effectively used her well-honed social skills to connect with industry leaders and peers. By really tuning in, throwing out thoughtful questions, and keeping in touch with her new connections, she expanded her network. This opened doors to new opportunities that took her career to the next level.

## Deepening Self-Knowledge

The journey to harnessing emotional intelligence starts within ourselves, employing strategies like self-awareness and self-regulation. As women professionals, gaining a deep understanding of our true selves is the cornerstone of confidently and adeptly managing our diverse roles and responsibilities.

Identifying and clarifying our core values is an essential first step in the introspective journey toward self-awareness and purposeful career growth. Engaging in exercises like value sorting or utilizing tools such as the Values in Action Inventory of Strengths (VIA-IS), Hogan Personality Assessment, DISC assessment, and CliftonStrengths can help us uncover the core principles that guide our decisions and actions. Each of these tools offers unique insights: while VIA-IS highlights personal strengths, Hogan focuses on personality traits, and DISC sheds light on behavioral tendencies. This multifaceted understanding enables us to approach challenging situations with integrity and resilience, keeping our actions aligned with our core values.

Authenticity in the workplace is about evolving alongside our roles and responsibilities. Embracing this dynamic authenticity allows us to adapt without compromising our values, enabling a sense of genuine self in all our professional endeavors.

Structured journaling is another powerful tool in our introspective toolkit. By documenting our responses to key workplace events and reflecting on specific questions—like "What emotional triggers surfaced for me today?" or "How did my feelings impact my decisions?"—we create a mirror to see our patterns and learn from them. This continuous self-dialogue is essential for recognizing our emotional responses and guiding our growth.

Seeking and analyzing feedback from trusted peers and mentors enriches this process. Specific, actionable insights from others provide an external perspective on how our emotional behaviors are perceived, offering opportunities for refinement and development.

It's crucial that we delve deeper into developing insight, which acts as a bridge connecting self-knowledge to its practical application. This transition from introspective discoveries to actionable wisdom is transformative. In my own practice, I often work with coaches to help unravel some of the blind spots that even seasoned professionals can miss. Engaging with a coach or therapist for guided self-reflection uncovers layers of our psyche that we often overlook by ourselves. This enhanced understanding significantly enriches our application of emotional intelligence in daily interactions.

As a coach, I've seen firsthand how invaluable certain tools can be in refining our emotional skills. Employing resources like 360-degree feedback, emotional intelligence assessments, and self-awareness questionnaires provides objective insights that are essential for growth. In my practice, I guide clients through these tools to gather actionable feedback, which helps us tailor personal and professional development plans.

This approach ensures that our growth is both intentional and measurable, making every step forward count.

Integrating mindfulness and meditation into our routine can profoundly impact our ability to manage emotions, especially under pressure. Techniques such as mindful breathing or body scans help ground us in the present, enabling us to approach workplace challenges with a calm and composed demeanor. Additionally, cognitive reappraisal—a technique that involves reinterpreting a situation to change its emotional impact—can transform how we perceive and react to feedback, shifting our perspective from defensive to growth-oriented.

## Embracing Calm

After working on self-awareness and regulation, I realized how important it is to tackle another crucial aspect of emotional intelligence: effective stress management. I used to let stress get the best of me—always feeling tense, which would eventually manifest physically. The constant pressure I put on myself led to all sorts of issues. My shoulders felt like they were carrying the weight of the world, and it wasn't long before that tension turned into persistent neck and back problems.

The headaches followed, often triggered by clenching my jaw without even realizing it. Like many of us, I was trying to juggle multiple roles, pushing myself to meet high expectations in every area of my life. This overwhelming stress, if not managed, can lead to burnout, affecting both our professional lives and our personal well-being too. It's a common challenge, and acknowledging its effects is the first step towards managing it effectively.

One common trap is suppressing our emotions to maintain a professional facade. This might seem effective in the short term but can lead to significant emotional repercussions over time. Similarly, struggling to set clear boundaries between our professional and personal lives can create an imbalance, making it harder to manage stress effectively.

Facing these challenges, let's delve into actionable strategies that have personally helped me manage stress more effectively. These techniques provide a solid framework for maintaining emotional equilibrium in our professional lives.

One approach I've found particularly helpful is keeping a thought record. This technique involves tracking negative thoughts as they arise, identifying any cognitive distortions, and challenging these thoughts with more balanced, evidence-based thinking. By regularly practicing this after stressful interactions or critical decisions, we can gain perspective and significantly reduce emotional reactivity.

Another fundamental aspect of stress management is mindfulness meditation. Dedicating 10-20 minutes daily to mindfulness can profoundly impact our ability to stay present and engage with our thoughts and emotions without judgment. Whether it's through guided sessions on apps like Headspace or Calm or through personal meditation practices, the benefits of mindfulness in managing stress are immense. Techniques such as deep breathing, progressive muscle relaxation, and visualization can be particularly effective during high-stress moments, such as before a crucial meeting or presentation.

Incorporating regular self-care into our schedules is equally vital. Taking care of ourselves often falls to the bottom of the priority list, especially for women who are typically focused on the well-being of others—be it family, friends, or colleagues. However, it's crucial to remember that just like the safety instructions on an airplane advise, you must "put on your own oxygen mask first before assisting others." Your health—both mental and physical—needs to come first, because only when you're well can you truly support those around you.

Treat regular self-care activities as indispensable appointments in your schedule, equivalent to crucial work meetings, to ensure it becomes an integral part of your routine. Whether it's a weekly yoga class, a monthly spa day, or simply setting aside time for a walk in nature, these moments are vital to your overall well-being. Committing to these practices ensures that you're taking the time to recharge, allowing you to face your responsibilities with renewed energy and a clearer mind.

Furthermore, exploring holistic health practices can offer additional support. Techniques like acupuncture, aromatherapy, and nutritional therapy can enhance our overall well-being. Consulting with holistic health practitioners to create a personalized wellness plan that includes regular treatments and practices is another layer of support that can help manage stress effectively.

## Leading with Heart: Empathy in Action

Following our exploration of stress management, it's vital to delve into another crucial facet of emotional intelligence:

empathy. For women in leadership, honing empathy can transform workplace dynamics, creating a more inclusive and supportive environment. Let's explore some actionable strategies to enhance our empathetic skills in professional settings.

Let's begin with the strategy of active listening. For us as women leaders, active listening is crucial. It means giving the speaker undivided attention and genuinely understanding the emotions behind their words. In practice, this requires focusing entirely on the conversation, making eye contact, and occasionally paraphrasing to ensure understanding. For instance, if a colleague expresses concerns about their workload, respond with empathy: "It sounds like you're quite overwhelmed with this project. Let's discuss how we can adjust your responsibilities."

Empathy in leadership involves actively inspiring a nurturing environment. Regularly engage in conversations that go beyond work, asking about personal well-being and professional challenges. Use empathetic leadership to motivate and inspire, acknowledging the pressures your team may face and offering support. For example, asking "What's been the most challenging part of your project so far, and how can I support you?" can open the door to meaningful conversations that enhance team solidarity.

Often, we find ourselves focusing predominantly on emotional empathy, which can sometimes lead us to absorb others' emotions too deeply, impacting our own well-being. To balance this, cognitive empathy allows us to understand others' perspectives without necessarily sharing their emotions. For example, when a team member expresses frustration about a new policy, acknowledging their feelings with a statement like, "I see why this might be upsetting for you," helps validate their concerns without overwhelming us emotionally.

Transitioning from understanding to action, compassionate empathy compels us to move beyond mere recognition of feelings to actively addressing them. Suppose a colleague is overwhelmed with their workload; an empathetic action would be to offer support, such as adjusting deadlines or redistributing tasks where feasible. This alleviates their stress and reinforces a culture of support and understanding within the team.

However, inspiring broader culture of empathy within our teams and organizations is equally critical. We can lead by example, demonstrating empathy in our interactions and advocating for its value in corporate settings. Encouraging empathy through organizational practices can include regular check-ins focused on emotional well-being and not just productivity, promoting training sessions on emotional intelligence, and integrating empathy into leadership development programs.

Moreover, the application of empathy analytics can be transformative. By employing tools that analyze the emotional content of communications, we can gain insights into the emotional climate of our organizations, identifying areas where empathetic communication is needed. This data-driven approach can help us tailor our strategies to create a more empathetic workplace environment.

Lastly, engaging in cross-functional projects exposes us to diverse perspectives and challenges across the organization, enhancing our empathetic understanding. Organizing workshops that encourage employees from different departments to collaborate on empathy-building exercises can deepen mutual understanding and improve team dynamics.

## Leading with Grace

### *The Indra Nooyi Example*

As we explore how emotional intelligence can shape successful professional journeys, it's enlightening to reflect on the stories of women leaders who've exemplified these qualities. Indra Nooyi's tenure at PepsiCo demonstrates the significant role emotional intelligence plays at the highest levels of corporate leadership.

Indra Nooyi's rise from Chennai, India, to the pinnacle of global business was driven by her strategic foresight coupled with a deep sense of empathy. After joining PepsiCo in 1994, Nooyi was instrumental in acquiring brands like Tropicana and Quaker Oats, guiding the company towards a health-focused product line.

What truly distinguished Nooyi's leadership was her personal touch. She sent handwritten notes to the parents of her executives, a gesture that expressed genuine appreciation and forged deep connections. This personal approach extended to inspiring a workplace that celebrated cultural diversity and encouraged employees to express their unique backgrounds, enhancing the sense of belonging and respect among the team.

During her tenure, Nooyi steered PepsiCo through significant changes, emphasizing healthier products and sustainability. Her leadership style—marked by clarity, empathy, and visionary communication—helped her team internalize and embrace these shifts. She demonstrated that emotional intelligence is about understanding and aligning the emotional currents of a team towards shared goals.

Nooyi's story is a powerful reminder for all of us, particularly women professionals, about the strength of leading with emotional intelligence—how it involves not just understanding and managing our own emotions but also engaging with others in ways that can profoundly influence our professional trajectory and leadership style.

## Mary Barra's Transformative Impact at General Motors

Following Indra Nooyi's inspiring example, let's explore the story of another trailblazing leader, Mary Barra, whose journey at General Motors (GM) exemplifies the profound influence of emotional intelligence in leadership. As the first woman to head a major global automaker, Barra's ascent to CEO in 2014 was both a personal triumph and a milestone for women in the automotive industry.

Starting as a co-op student in 1980, Mary Barra's deep roots in GM equipped her with invaluable insights into the company's operations and culture. This extensive background informed her leadership style, marked by a strong emotional intelligence that she wielded to spearhead a cultural overhaul within the company.

Faced with GM's entrenched hierarchical culture, Barra initiated changes that emphasized open communication, transparency, and accountability. She understood that for GM to evolve, it needed to foster an environment where every employee felt heard and valued. By promoting these values, she enhanced internal collaboration and helped pivot the company towards a more dynamic and responsive organizational structure.

Barra's leadership faced a severe test early in her tenure during the 2014 ignition switch recall crisis, a daunting challenge with severe safety issues linked to fatalities. Displaying remarkable accountability and empathy, Barra took full responsibility. She addressed the public and the victims' families with heartfelt apologies and a firm commitment to rectify the mistakes. Her transparent and compassionate handling of the crisis restored public trust in GM and underscored the critical role of empathetic leadership in crisis management.

Moreover, Barra has been a staunch advocate for diversity and inclusion within GM. She has actively worked to increase the representation of women and minorities in leadership roles, firmly believing that a diverse leadership team inspires a more inclusive corporate culture. Under her direction, GM has received accolades for its commitment to gender equality and inclusivity.

Mary Barra's leadership at GM highlights how emotional intelligence can revolutionize a company's culture and operational success. Her approach—balancing empathetic leadership with decisive action—demonstrates that emotional intelligence is indispensable in modern corporate governance.

These examples show us that emotional intelligence is a practical toolkit for tackling daily interactions and long-term challenges.

Now, it's your turn. I encourage each one of you to start small in your journey to enhance your emotional intelligence. Consider applying just one of the emotional intelligence strategies we've explored in your next interaction at work. Whether it's practicing active listening, managing your responses with greater self-regulation, or simply taking a moment to understand a colleague's perspective, each small step is a leap towards becoming a more empathetic and effective leader.

# CHAPTER 3

# FINANCIALLY FORWARD: BUILDING YOUR ECONOMIC INDEPENDENCE

Falguni Nayar, the founder of Nykaa, once said, *"As women, we need to take charge of our financial future. We need to educate ourselves about money, invest wisely, and make smart financial decisions that will help us achieve our goals and aspirations."* Her words strike a chord with me because they highlight a truth that has often been overlooked: the critical importance of financial independence for women.

For too long, many societies, including ours in India, have placed women in roles that limit their financial autonomy. Traditionally, women have been expected to be caregivers and homemakers, while the responsibility of managing finances fell to the men. This mindset has perpetuated the belief that women are not capable of handling financial matters or making significant financial decisions. Factors such as limited access to education, fewer job opportunities, workplace discrimination, and ingrained cultural expectations have further reinforced this narrative, keeping women from fully realizing their financial potential.

But the tides are changing. Women are beginning to recognize the importance of taking control of their financial destinies, and it's a movement that's gaining momentum.

The call for women to take control of their financial future has never been more urgent. Around the globe, the gender pay gap persists as a formidable barrier, directly impacting women's financial autonomy and long-term security. In India, for instance, the disparity is striking. According to the Periodic Labour Force Surveys (PLFS) of 2023, male regular wage workers earned 24% more than female workers in 2023. This gap is even more glaring among the self-employed, where men earn nearly three times more than women. These numbers reflect deeply rooted societal norms and the lack of representation of women in higher-paying roles. And as women advance in their careers, this gap only seems to widen.

This issue isn't confined to India. If we look at the UK, progress has been slow. As of 2023, the gender pay gap for full-time employees was 7.7%, with men earning more across all major occupational groups. The disparity is even greater among higher earners, where the top 10% of male earners made nearly 15% more than their female counterparts, according to the Annual Survey for Hours and Earnings (ASHE) in 2023.

Meanwhile, in the United States, the gender pay gap has stubbornly remained stagnant for the past two decades. Women earned about 82 cents for every dollar earned by men in 2022, according to research from The Pew Research Center.

These numbers starkly remind us of the challenges women face in achieving financial independence. They underscore the importance of understanding these disparities and actively working to overcome them.

Financial independence is more than just a buzzword for women professionals—it's a necessity, especially in workplaces where this gender pay gap looms large. This independence is about reclaiming power in a world that often undervalues women's contributions. It enables women to make choices that align with their passions and ambitions, opening doors to career opportunities that might otherwise be out of reach. Financial security also ensures peace of mind. The stress and anxiety that come with financial uncertainty can take a heavy toll, not just on women themselves but also on their families. When women are financially secure, they can focus more on their goals, their well-being, and their personal growth.

Financially independent women become trailblazers, setting examples for future generations, and showing them that they, too, can break through the barriers that have long held women back.

Let me tell you about Maya, an inspiring professional I've had the privilege of working with. Maya's story is one of resilience and determination. She grew up in a small town in India, where the traditional gender roles often dictated what women could and couldn't do. But Maya wasn't content with the limited paths available to her. She had a vision of a future where she was both financially independent and professionally successful, a vision that many around her found difficult to comprehend.

Maya's early career was a wake-up call to the harsh realities of the gender pay gap. Working in a male-dominated engineering firm, she quickly noticed that her male colleagues were earning more for doing the same work. It wasn't just a one-off; this disparity was a systemic issue that stretched across the industry. Maya knew she couldn't let this slide if she wanted to achieve her goals. She decided to take control of her financial future, determined to level the playing field.

Her journey began with financial literacy. Maya attended every workshop and online course she could find on budgeting, saving, and investing. She was committed to understanding the complexities of managing money, setting clear financial goals like saving a specific percentage of her income and venturing into investments in mutual funds and stocks. As her financial knowledge grew, so did her confidence, and soon, she saw her savings and investments begin to multiply.

Balancing her career with family responsibilities was another challenge Maya faced, one familiar to many women. When she took a break for maternity leave, she was acutely aware of the long-term financial impact it could have. But Maya had planned ahead. She had built an emergency fund and continued contributing to her savings even during her break.

Coming back to the office, Maya was more determined than ever to close the pay gap. With her newfound financial confidence and armed with data, she boldly negotiated a salary increase. She took on leadership roles that allowed her to showcase her skills, and her efforts didn't go unnoticed. Soon, she was leading major projects, earning a better paycheck and the respect of her peers.

Maya's journey to financial independence transformed her as a source of inspiration for other women around her. She became a vocal advocate for financial literacy and independence, going as far as starting a mentorship program at her workplace aimed at guiding young female professionals through the hurdles she once encountered. Her story is an example of the incredible things that can happen when women take charge of their financial futures.

True financial independence equips women with the resources and savvy needed to make choices that align with their personal ambitions and professional objectives. It's about smart money management—saving with purpose, investing with insight, and planning with precision. This kind of independence is liberating. It transforms financial resources from mere means of survival into tools for achieving long-term goals.

To truly embrace this transformative power, there's a need for a shift in mindset—one that recognizes both the challenges and opportunities unique to women. For too long, societal norms have positioned men as the primary financial decision-makers. This has left many women relying on male family members for financial management, perpetuating a cycle of dependency. But as more women enter the workforce and contribute significantly to household incomes, it becomes increasingly vital that their economic contributions translate into personal financial empowerment.

This shift isn't just about dollars and cents—it's about confidence and self-efficacy. Many women, shaped by societal conditioning, doubt their abilities to make sound financial decisions. But embracing a mindset of financial independence can boost confidence, helping women take control of their financial futures and break the stereotypes that suggest they're less capable of handling finances. This is about asserting that financial literacy and decision-making are essential skills for everyone, regardless of gender.

Financial independence also plays a critical role in personal and family security. Life's uncertainties can be less daunting when you've taken charge of your finances. Women who manage their finances are better prepared to handle these situations without undue hardship, providing a safety net for themselves and their loved ones. Moreover, financially independent women can pass on their knowledge and skills to future generations, creating a culture of financial literacy and independence within their families.

The empowerment and autonomy that come with financial independence extend far beyond personal security. Financial independence also enhances a woman's negotiating power, whether in salary discussions at work or financial decisions at home, strengthening her position in both personal and professional settings.

Finally, the impact of financially independent women reaches into the broader economy and society. When women manage their finances effectively, they contribute to economic growth, investing in their communities and supporting local economies. And as more women gain financial independence, they're in a stronger position to advocate for social change, supporting initiatives that promote gender equality and financial literacy for all.

However, achieving this independence often requires overcoming some common hurdles. One significant barrier is the hesitation to invest. Many women, possibly daunted by perceived risks or unclear about their options, tend to stash their savings in low-yield accounts rather than seeking investment opportunities that could significantly increase their wealth through compound interest. Engaging with different investment avenues—be it stocks, mutual funds, or real estate—tailored to personal risk tolerance and financial goals, is essential for financial growth.

Another stumbling block is the tendency to procrastinate on financial planning. Waiting for the 'right' financial moment before starting to manage money is a common pitfall. This delay can result in missed opportunities for accumulating savings and harnessing the growth potential of investments.

## Foundations of Financial Health

In my experience, one of the most empowering steps a woman can take toward financial independence is learning to budget effectively. Budgeting helps you get a crystal-clear view of your finances, enabling you to make choices that take care of what you need now and what you're aiming for down the line.

When you create a budget, you're giving yourself the gift of clarity. It's like taking a deep breath and finally seeing all the pieces of your financial puzzle laid out before you. You can see where your money is coming from, where it's going, and, most importantly, where it might be slipping through the cracks. This awareness is especially crucial for women who might face fluctuating income due to career breaks or part-time work.

By understanding your financial picture, you gain control. You're no longer just reacting to expenses as they come; you're making informed decisions about how to allocate your money. Maybe you realize you're spending more on takeout than you thought, or perhaps you see that you could be saving more if you adjusted a few habits. This kind of insight is what helps you align your spending with what truly matters to you—whether that's building an emergency fund, investing in your future, or just having a little more peace of mind.

Budgeting also reduces stress. There's something incredibly reassuring about knowing you have a plan in place, that every penny has a purpose. It allows you to feel secure, even when life throws unexpected expenses your way. And with this sense of security comes the confidence to make strategic financial decisions that can lead to long-term stability and independence.

After establishing a solid budget, the next step is setting clear financial goals. This is about aligning your money with your life's aspirations. Whether you're saving for that dream home, planning to further your education, or eyeing a business venture, setting specific financial goals helps ensure your hard-earned money is working towards what truly matters to you.

For many women, these goals represent a pathway to greater freedom and independence. By thoughtfully integrating your career ambitions into your financial planning, you create a roadmap that supports both personal fulfillment and professional growth. This process keeps you on track to achieve specific objectives and deepens your financial literacy, empowering you to tackle the often complex financial decisions with greater confidence.

Equally important is preparing for the unexpected with an emergency fund. Life is full of surprises, and this fund acts as your financial shock absorber, providing peace of mind during sudden personal crises or global economic downturns. For women, who often face unique financial challenges such as the gender pay gap or potential career interruptions, having this safety net is indispensable. It allows you the freedom to pursue your career goals without the constant worry of financial fallback, empowering you to take calculated risks that can lead to significant professional growth and personal satisfaction.

## Money-Smart Moves

As a coach who works closely with many ambitious women in various fields, I often encounter the pressing question: How does one start with effective budgeting? Drawing from my own experiences and the lessons I've shared with others, here's how we can break it down into manageable steps.

Before anything, it's vital to get a clear picture of where your money comes from and where it's going. Many of us juggle multiple roles—perhaps you're balancing a full-time job with freelance gigs, or you're venturing into a side business. It's crucial to consolidate all these income streams to understand your total earnings. This holistic view is especially important if you're navigating periods like maternity leave or sabbaticals, where you might lean more on these alternative sources.

Next, selecting a budgeting method that complements the unique rhythm of your career is key. The 50/30/20 rule, for instance, offers a structured yet flexible framework ideal for those with fluctuating incomes. This rule suggests allocating 50% of your after-tax income to necessities, 30% to wants, and 20% towards savings and debt repayment. Its simplicity and clear categorization make it a favorite among financial advisors for its ease of adoption and maintenance.

For those of us who need to squeeze the most out of every rupee, zero-based budgeting can be a game-changer. This method involves assigning every rupee a job, from rent and groceries to savings and entertainment, ensuring there's no wastage. It's perfect for periods when every penny counts, such as during a career transition or when planning for a major life event.

But it's not just about the here and now. Long-term financial security is equally important. For women, who statistically live longer than men, planning for retirement needs to be a top priority. This means contributing to a retirement fund and considering investments in diverse asset classes that can grow and provide for you in the years to come. The goal is to create a financial cushion that allows you to live comfortably post-career, free from the worry of financial instability.

To keep everything on track, technology can be your best friend. With so many budgeting apps available, managing your finances can become a part of your routine. These tools can automate expense tracking, provide real-time insights, and even help you spot patterns in your spending that might need adjustment. Regularly reviewing your spending is a habit worth cultivating—it's your way of staying accountable to yourself and your goals. By keeping an eye on where your money is going, you can ensure that every penny is working toward something that truly matters to you.

Life has a way of throwing unexpected changes our way, and when it comes to our finances, adaptability is key. I remember when I transitioned to a new job with a completely different benefits package; suddenly, I had to rethink how I managed my health insurance and retirement contributions. Adjusting my budget to reflect these changes entailed ensuring my financial plan continued to support my evolving personal and professional goals.

## Buffer Your Budget: Building an Emergency Fund

This brings us to another critical aspect of financial planning: building an emergency fund. It involves creating a financial safety net that allows you to tackle life's uncertainties without losing momentum on your long-term goals. Whether you're facing an unexpected job loss, taking a career break to focus on family, or dealing with the challenges of workplace discrimination, having an emergency fund can be the difference between making a choice out of necessity and making one out of ambition.

Having this financial cushion empowers us. It gives us the freedom to explore opportunities that match our career aspirations and personal values, rather than feeling pressured into decisions by financial constraints. This is the kind of security that allows for true professional growth and personal peace of mind.

When I first decided to prioritize my emergency fund, I started by clearly understanding my regular expenses. It was all about knowing how much I needed monthly for the essentials like housing, utilities, and groceries. My target was to cover at least six months of these expenses. For those of us with fluctuating incomes, like freelancers or consultants, it might be a good idea to aim for even more, perhaps up to a year.

I found breaking this big goal into smaller chunks incredibly helpful. Rather than getting overwhelmed by the total sum, I focused on setting aside smaller amounts regularly. This made the goal feel more attainable and less daunting.

Automating your savings can be particularly effective. Setting up automatic transfers from your checking account to a dedicated emergency savings account ensures that you consistently contribute without needing to think about it. Many people find that allocating a portion of their paycheck to go directly into their savings is an easy way to prioritize this goal.

Using financial apps that round up your purchases and transfer the difference to your savings account is another simple method to help your fund grow. It's a small step that doesn't impact your day-to-day budget much but can accumulate significantly over time.

As you work on building your emergency fund, it's equally important to keep an eye on high-interest debt. Balancing both can seem challenging, but it's a crucial step toward long-term financial stability. Tackling debt while saving ensures that you're not just setting money aside, but also freeing up future income that would otherwise go toward interest payments.

One approach that has worked well for many is to prioritize paying down high-interest debt, like credit cards, alongside building your emergency fund. This is where strategies like the debt snowball or debt avalanche methods come into play. The debt snowball method involves paying off your smallest debts first, which can give you a psychological boost as you see debts disappear. The debt avalanche method, on the other hand, targets the highest-interest debts first, saving you more money on interest over time.

Another key aspect is reevaluating and adjusting your plan as you go. Regular financial check-ins can help ensure your savings strategy aligns with your current goals. Life is always changing, whether it's a salary increase, a new job, or unexpected expenses. These shifts may require you to adjust your contributions or even reconsider your priorities.

As your financial situation improves, it's a good idea to increase your monthly savings. Even small, incremental increases can have a significant impact on the growth of your emergency fund over time.

And if you ever need to tap into your emergency fund, make replenishing it a priority. This might mean increasing your savings temporarily or cutting back in other areas until your fund is back to its target level. This habit ensures that your financial safety net remains intact, ready to support you through future challenges.

## The Transformative Power of Investing

When we're laying down the groundwork for financial freedom, it's key to remember it's not just about saving and sticking to a budget. It's also about making your money hustle for you. This is where investing comes into play—an essential strategy for growing your wealth and securing your future. But I know that for many of us, the idea of investing can feel intimidating. However, with the right approach, investing can be both manageable and rewarding, especially when tailored to the unique challenges and opportunities we face.

For women in their 20s and early 30s, this is a time to embrace an aggressive growth strategy. The advantage of being early in your career is that you have time on your side. This means you can afford to take on more risk with the potential for higher returns. One of the most effective ways to do this is by focusing on equities—stocks or equity mutual funds that can offer significant capital appreciation over time.

But it's not just about jumping into the stock market; it's about building a diversified portfolio. Diversification means spreading your investments across different types of assets to reduce risk. For instance, a mix of domestic and international stocks, along with small-cap and large-cap equities, can help capture growth across various market segments. This way, if one area underperforms, others can help balance out your portfolio.

I've noticed that a prevalent mistake among young women is shying away from equities due to a perceived risk. It's easy to feel cautious, especially when you hear about market downturns or financial losses. But the beauty of starting young is that you have a long investment horizon, giving you the ability to recover from market dips. Understanding this can help you feel more confident in making riskier investments that have the potential for greater rewards.

Another pitfall to watch out for is underutilizing employer benefits. Many women don't maximize their contributions to employer-sponsored retirement plans, which can be a missed opportunity. These plans often come with employer matches and tax advantages, which are essentially savings that shouldn't be left on the table.

It's essential to continually educate yourself about financial markets and investment opportunities. Through my interactions with numerous professionals, I've observed that many women experience a significant boost in confidence regarding investment decisions when they enhance their financial literacy. Leveraging resources such as online courses, financial advisors, and user-friendly investment apps can demystify the complexities of investing. These tools provide the support and insights needed to make informed decisions, enhancing your ability to manage and grow your investments effectively.

It is important to recognize that as life evolves, so too should your investment approach. As you transition into your 30s and 40s, the responsibilities you carry—whether it's family, a mortgage, or career growth—start to shape your financial priorities. This is where a balanced investment strategy becomes crucial, blending growth with the stability needed to tackle these new phases.

This means diversifying your portfolio to include a mix of assets—equities for growth and fixed-income securities for stability. This blend ensures that while you're still pursuing growth, you're also safeguarding your investments against potential market volatility. A popular choice here is target date funds, which automatically adjust your asset allocation as you approach retirement. It's a hands-off way to maintain balance, providing peace of mind as you focus on other aspects of your life.

However, a common pitfall at this stage is the tendency to become overly conservative. As responsibilities mount, it's natural to lean towards safer, low-risk investments like bonds. While these offer stability, they can also limit your growth potential. It's about finding that sweet spot where your investments are both secure and poised for growth. Similarly, ensuring your portfolio is well-diversified across various asset classes is crucial. Failing to do so can expose you to unnecessary risk and diminish your returns over time.

Addressing these challenges means regularly reassessing your risk tolerance. Life changes may prompt a shift in your financial goals and responsibilities, necessitating adjustments to your investment strategy to ensure it continues to meet your needs. Consulting with a financial advisor can be invaluable in this process, helping you create and maintain a diversified portfolio that balances growth with security.

It is essential to pivot gracefully as you approach the later stages of your professional life. This stage of life calls for a strategy that emphasizes stability and capital preservation, ensuring that the hard-earned wealth you've accumulated over the years is secure while still providing a steady income stream.

One effective way to achieve this is by gradually increasing your allocation to fixed-income securities, such as bonds. Unlike stocks, which can be volatile, bonds typically offer more predictable returns and lower risk, making them an attractive option as you near retirement. This shift helps to safeguard your investments, providing a reliable source of income during your retirement years while protecting your principal.

However, even with a more conservative strategy, it's important to avoid the pitfall of neglecting regular portfolio rebalancing. Market conditions and personal circumstances change over time, and your investment portfolio should reflect these changes. Failing to rebalance can inadvertently expose you to risks you may no longer be comfortable with. Regular reviews of your portfolio allow you to adjust your asset allocation to ensure it continues to align with your financial goals and evolving risk tolerance.

In this stage of life, conducting these portfolio reviews becomes both a financial exercise and a way to maintain peace of mind. It's about securing a future where you can enjoy the fruits of your labor, free from financial stress, and focused on what truly matters to you.

## Mastering Diversification for Financial Empowerment

It is time to take a closer look at something we've touched on in these pages: the importance of diversification in your investment portfolio. Diversification serves as a crucial strategy for mitigating risk and enhancing the opportunity for consistent growth.

Think about this: you've diligently invested in a few sectors you're familiar with, perhaps in industries where you've worked or have some insight. While this may feel comfortable, it also leaves you vulnerable if those specific sectors face downturns. That's where diversification steps in. By spreading your investments across various asset classes—stocks, bonds, real estate, and even international markets—you reduce the risk that any single downturn could severely impact your overall portfolio.

However, I often encounter women who hesitate to diversify or seek professional financial advice. Whether it's due to a lack of confidence or concerns about the cost, many women miss out on the benefits that come with expert guidance. In my conversations with friends, peers, and the women I coach, I emphasize the value of engaging with a financial advisor. These professionals can help tailor an investment strategy that aligns with your specific goals and circumstances, ensuring you're both diversified and optimized for growth.

Another critical aspect to consider is your risk tolerance and financial goals. Risk tolerance is highly personal and can change over time. A young professional just starting out might feel comfortable taking on more risk, given the long time horizon to recover from market fluctuations. On the other hand, if you're approaching retirement, your focus may shift towards preserving capital, making a more conservative approach appealing.

Defining your financial goals is equally important. By clearly outlining what you want to achieve, you can ensure that your portfolio is working towards those goals, providing both peace of mind and a clear path forward.

When thinking about how to diversify your investments, it's wise to consider a mix of asset types that go beyond the traditional. Real estate and commodities, for example, can provide an additional layer of security. Investing in real estate—whether directly or through other means—can offer exposure to the property market, while commodities like gold serve as a hedge against inflation. These types of investments help ensure your portfolio isn't overly dependent on any single asset, offering a broader base of financial stability.

It's also important to remember that not all investments need to be long-term. Short-term options, such as certain savings instruments or similar low-risk avenues, offer liquidity and safety. These are ideal for setting aside money for emergencies or other short-term financial needs, ensuring that you have cash on hand when you need it most without having to dip into your long-term investments during unfavorable market conditions.

Another key aspect of building a resilient portfolio is to think about diversification across different sectors and regions. By spreading your investments across industries like technology, healthcare, and consumer goods, you reduce the risk that comes from being too heavily invested in any single sector. Similarly, investing in various geographic regions can protect your portfolio against country-specific risks and currency fluctuations, allowing you to tap into global opportunities and smooth out potential market volatility.

Choosing investment vehicles that keep costs low is also essential for maximizing your returns. Options that provide broad market exposure without the high fees often associated with active management are a practical choice. And while building your portfolio, it's crucial to think about the long term—setting aside funds specifically for retirement, leveraging the power of compound growth over time, and taking advantage of tax-efficient strategies that can help you keep more of what you earn .

But the work doesn't stop at investing. To ensure that your investments remain on target with your financial goals and adapt to life's inevitable changes, regular portfolio reviews are essential. These reviews can help you assess whether your investments are still aligned with your financial goals, especially after significant life events like a career change or the addition of a new family member. This practice keeps your financial strategy responsive and dynamic.

Rebalancing your portfolio is just as crucial. This process involves adjusting your holdings to maintain your desired level of risk and asset allocation. If some investments have performed well and now represent a larger portion of your portfolio than intended, it might be time to sell some of these assets to reinvest in others that have not performed as well, thus maintaining a balanced approach. Regular rebalancing helps in mitigating risk and ensuring that your investment strategy continues to reflect your current financial situation and future aspirations.

As you integrate these strategies, remember that your financial journey is unique to you. It's about making informed choices that reflect your personal circumstances, goals, and aspirations. The more you engage with and understand your investments, the more empowered you will feel in taking control of your financial future.

## Planning for Tomorrow:  A Smart Start to Retirement Planning

Let's not overlook the cornerstone of long-term stability—retirement planning. It's easy to push this to the back burner when you're juggling day-to-day demands, but laying the groundwork early can transform your golden years from a period of uncertainty to one of comfort and security.

Retirement planning is a vital aspect of financial security, particularly for women who face unique challenges in the workplace. The key is to start early, taking advantage of the power of compounding—where even small, regular savings can grow into significant sums over time. The earlier you begin, the more you can maximize this compounding effect, which can turn modest contributions into a substantial nest egg for the future.

I've noticed that even today, many women still lean on someone else, like a brother, dad, or husband, to manage their money matters. But, honestly, it's vital to take charge of your own finances. When you start handling your own savings and investments, you're securing your financial freedom, boosting your confidence and arming yourself with the know-how to make smart choices for your future.

One effective strategy is to start saving as soon as you begin your career. Set aside a portion of your income regularly, and consider reinvesting any earnings to further accelerate growth. As your career progresses, you can adapt your investment strategies to align with your evolving financial goals, whether that's saving for a home, a child's education, or retirement.

Additionally, think about how you can contribute more aggressively to your retirement savings, especially in the early stages of your career. Whenever you receive a bonus or other financial windfall, consider investing it rather than spending it. This habit of consistently saving and investing will pay off significantly in the long run, providing you with security and freedom.

It is also important to consider additional layers of protection to enhance your safety net. Early in your career, you might focus on growth by directing a significant portion of your investments into higher-risk, higher-reward options like equities. As you approach retirement, gradually shifting your focus towards more conservative investments can help balance growth with security, ensuring that your nest egg is well-protected against market fluctuations.

Tax planning is another critical piece of the retirement puzzle. Developing a strategy for tax-efficient withdrawals can significantly impact the longevity of your retirement savings. By understanding how different withdrawal strategies affect your tax liability, you can make informed decisions that minimize taxes and maximize income during your retirement years.

It's also worthwhile to explore your country's financial policies and schemes, especially those tailored for women. Some countries offer special tax rebates, lower loan rates, or specific pension plans designed to benefit women. By leveraging these opportunities, you can optimize your financial strategy to better suit your personal needs and long-term goals. Take the time to research and understand these benefits, as they can make a significant difference in building a secure financial future.

But let's not overlook healthcare—a paramount concern as we age. Integrating a solid healthcare plan into your retirement strategy is vital. Investing in comprehensive health insurance that covers a range of medical needs, from critical illnesses to routine care, will protect you against unforeseen medical costs. Additionally, establishing a dedicated healthcare fund within your retirement portfolio ensures you have ready access to funds for medical emergencies, invested in assets that provide both safety and liquidity.

Lastly, regular financial health check-ups are crucial. Just as we periodically reassess our physical health, reviewing financial plans annually with your advisor ensures your retirement strategy remains aligned with your current life stage and financial goals. This proactive approach allows you to adjust your plans in response to life's changes, ensuring your retirement plan is as dynamic as life itself.

The strategies we've discussed won't make a difference unless you begin implementing them in your life. It's time to move from understanding to doing. So, I challenge you: identify one financial aspect you've perhaps overlooked or felt too intimidated to tackle. Set a goal for this month. It could be as simple as understanding your current retirement contributions or as ambitious as setting up a diversified investment portfolio. Whatever you choose, commit to taking that first step. Share your goals with a friend, a mentor, or even jot them down in your journal. Accountability can transform intention into action.

Start today. Your future self will thank you.

# CHAPTER 4

# NEVER STOP GROWING: UPSKILLING FOR TODAY AND TOMORROW

Indra Nooyi, former CEO of PepsiCo, once said something that has stayed with me over the years: *"The only way you're going to achieve what you want is to be a lifelong student. Study everything."* Those words have inspired me and given me a clear direction in my own path of growth and learning.

This philosophy of continuous learning is embodied in the journey of Ayesha, a female engineer I met who carved out a successful career in a male-dominated industry. Early on, Ayesha recognized that if she wanted to break through the glass ceiling and tackle the challenges of gender bias, she needed to embrace lifelong learning. But this wasn't just about collecting qualifications—it was about building her authority, credibility, and presence in an industry where those qualities were often questioned simply because of her gender.

Ayesha's commitment to learning became her superpower. She didn't settle for what she already knew; she actively sought out opportunities to expand her knowledge. Enrolling in professional courses and workshops, Ayesha sharpened her technical skills and stayed on top of the latest trends in her field. This dedication to continuous education was crucial—it kept her competitive, relevant, and respected in a fast-evolving industry.

Ayesha understood that thriving in her field required more than just technical know-how. She focused on building her emotional intelligence (EQ) and decency quotient (DQ)—skills that are often overlooked but are crucial in navigating workplace dynamics. By honing these abilities, Ayesha was able to foster stronger relationships with her colleagues and create an environment where respect was the norm, not the exception.

In male-dominated fields, women often face biases and stereotypes that can undermine their confidence and career progress. Ayesha wasn't immune to these challenges; there were moments when her capabilities were questioned simply because of her gender. But rather than letting these setbacks define her, she used them as fuel to push forward. Her commitment to lifelong learning wasn't just about gaining knowledge—it was about equipping herself to meet these challenges head-on.

One of the philosophies Ayesha embraced was "sharpening the axe." This idea, rooted in the concept of working smarter rather than harder, was a game-changer for her. Instead of just grinding through tasks, she took the time to learn and refine her skills, ensuring that she could approach problems with a sharp mind and a clear strategy. This approach boosted her efficiency and demonstrated her commitment to excellence—a quality that didn't go unnoticed by her peers and superiors.

## The Lifelong Learner

Ayesha's journey underscores the necessity of continuous learning, especially for women in evolving industries. In today's swiftly changing world, often described as VUCA—volatile, uncertain, complex, and ambiguous—staying still isn't an option. For us women professionals, continuous learning is a lifeline, a way to stay relevant and competitive in environments that are constantly shifting.

One of the unique advantages of continuous learning for women in the workplace is that it helps us stay ahead of the curve. As industries evolve, acquiring new skills and knowledge becomes essential. Whether it's understanding the latest technology, mastering new tools, or adapting to changing market demands, continuous learning ensures that we are always prepared to take on new roles and responsibilities. This enhances our career prospects and gives us the confidence to step into leadership positions.

In industries where leadership roles are often dominated by men, upskilling is a powerful tool for breaking through barriers. By focusing on high-demand areas like artificial intelligence (AI) and digital leadership, women can equip themselves with the skills needed to challenge the status quo and advance into positions of influence.

Engaging in learning and development (L&D) opportunities also has a profound impact on job security and personal growth. As women, when we commit to continuous learning, we boost our confidence, enhance our performance, and open doors to new opportunities. This empowerment is crucial, especially when tackling the challenges of the workplace.

Moreover, the ability to adapt to market changes is vital for long-term career success. Continuous learning makes us more resilient, better prepared for shifts in the job market, and ready to seize new opportunities as they arise.

Empowering women through upskilling also has a significant economic impact. A McKinsey Global Institute report suggests that increasing women's participation in the labor force could boost global GDP by $12 trillion by 2025. This highlights the untapped potential that we, as women, hold in shaping economic trajectories, and it all starts with a commitment to never stop learning.

On the path to continuous learning and upskilling, we face both systemic obstacles and self-imposed hurdles. I've seen this firsthand.  I've often heard from women in my coaching sessions about the frustration of having fewer opportunities for professional development compared to their male colleagues. It's not just about being passed over; it's about the subtle biases that influence who gets selected for training. These stereotypes about our roles and capabilities can create a real barrier, leaving talented women without the resources they need to grow.

And then there's the juggling act we're all too familiar with—balancing work and personal responsibilities. For many of us, especially those managing caregiving duties, finding the time to upskill can feel like trying to fit a square peg in a round hole. It's not just about squeezing in time; it's about making that time meaningful and productive.

I've seen firsthand how the lack of female mentors in male-dominated fields can make this even tougher. Mentorship is so important for professional development. It's not just about guidance; it's about having someone who gets where you're coming from and can help you navigate the challenges you're facing. Without that support, it can feel like you're trying to climb a mountain without the right gear.

And then there's the issue of financial constraints. We know how expensive courses, certifications, and other learning resources can be. When you're already earning less than your male counterparts, it's easy to see how this becomes a significant barrier. Many women I've worked with have had to make tough choices between immediate needs and long-term career investments, and it can feel like you're stuck in a catch-22.

Beyond the systemic challenges we face, there are also the self-imposed barriers that can hold us back. I've seen this time and again in my coaching sessions—women who are incredibly capable but find themselves stuck because of certain mindsets or fears. One of the biggest hurdles is the fixed mindset, where we start believing that our abilities are set in stone, that we're either good at something or we're not, and there's no room for growth.

It's easy to fall into the trap of self-doubt, thinking that we don't belong in certain roles or industries. But I've learned—and I've seen others learn—that these doubts are often unfounded. Our abilities aren't static; they can grow and evolve with the right mindset and effort. The key is to recognize this and push beyond the comfort zone, to embrace challenges rather than shy away from them.

Another pitfall I've noticed is when upskilling efforts aren't aligned with broader career objectives or organizational goals. It's not uncommon to see someone diving into courses or certifications without a clear sense of how it fits into their overall career plan. This can lead to wasted time and resources, not to mention missed opportunities for advancement. It's crucial to set clear, measurable learning goals that are in sync with both your personal aspirations and the needs of your organization. This alignment ensures that your efforts are targeted and effective, driving you toward your ultimate goals.

Then there's the underutilization of support networks—an area where many of us could improve. Mentorship and networking are incredibly powerful tools for career development. They provide guidance, open doors to new opportunities, and offer the encouragement we need to keep pushing forward. Yet, I've seen many women hesitate to fully leverage these networks, either because they don't want to impose or because they don't realize the value of these relationships. But mentors can offer perspectives and insights that we might not see on our own, helping us navigate challenges and build a growth mindset.

And let's not forget the fear of failure—a barrier that can be particularly paralyzing. I've worked with women who are so afraid of making mistakes that they avoid taking risks altogether. But here's the thing: growth often comes from stepping outside our comfort zones, from taking on challenges that stretch us.

To truly unlock the full potential of continuous learning and development, it's crucial to tackle these systemic and self-imposed barriers. This is where embracing a growth mindset can make all the difference.

## Paving the Path to Opportunity with a Growth Mindset

For women professionals, the importance of embracing a growth mindset cannot be overstated. It is about transforming how we approach every challenge, setback, and opportunity in our careers.

One of the most tangible ways to imbibe a growth mindset is by embracing challenges rather than shying away from them. We've all faced moments when a task seemed daunting, perhaps even impossible. But what if, instead of viewing these challenges as roadblocks, we saw them as opportunities? Opportunities to stretch our capabilities, innovate, and learn something new. Taking on a challenging project, for example, can be transformative. It pushes us to step outside our comfort zones, apply fresh strategies, and, in many cases, achieve results that far exceed our own expectations.

When I talk about the need for a growth mindset, I'm reminded of a personal experience early in my career. There was a promotion I was really hoping for, but I missed out on it because I didn't have a specific certification. I can still recall the frustration. I could have taken that certification earlier, but I had decided not to, thinking the organization should invest in it for me. Someone else, who had already earned that certification, ended up getting the role.

That moment was a wake-up call. I realized that waiting for others to provide opportunities for growth wasn't serving me. Since then, I've made it a priority to invest in my own development, regardless of whether the company offers support. Every year, I set aside a portion of my income specifically for learning, and I've committed to adding at least one new skill to my résumé annually.

Over time, I've earned several certifications—PCC ICF, Hogan, ATD, MBTI, Hays job certification, and more. These qualifications didn't just add to my résumé; they gave me an edge. I began to notice how these skills gave me more confidence and leverage in negotiations for better roles, higher-level responsibilities, and new career opportunities.

Approaching challenges with this mindset of continuous learning and self-improvement has transformed my career. By tackling obstacles head-on and using them as opportunities to grow, I've been able to shape my own path. This is the power of a growth mindset—it allows us to see every challenge as a stepping stone toward something greater.

By adopting this mindset, we start breaking down barriers and unlocking new possibilities in our careers. It's about embracing those challenges as catalysts for growth and transformation.

Learning from setbacks is another critical aspect of the growth mindset. In a rapidly changing work environment, setbacks are inevitable. But instead of viewing them as failures, we can see them as valuable feedback. What went wrong? Why did it happen? What can be done differently next time? By analyzing these questions, we can identify areas for improvement and adjust our strategies accordingly. This approach inspires resilience but also adaptability, two traits that are essential for long-term success.

Building resilience is about more than just bouncing back from failures—it's about using those experiences as stepping stones for future success. Every setback offers a lesson, and every lesson learned makes us stronger and more prepared for the challenges ahead. This is the essence of a growth mindset: understanding that growth is a continuous process, shaped by our experiences and how we respond to them.

Promoting self-determined learning is another key component of this mindset. Taking ownership of our professional development is empowering. It's about being proactive in seeking out resources, setting personal learning objectives, and actively pursuing opportunities to expand our knowledge and skills. This self-directed approach to learning enhances our career prospects and gives us a greater sense of control over our professional journey.

Embracing a growth mindset entails both professional development and personal empowerment. It's about believing in our ability to grow, adapt, and succeed, no matter the challenges we face.

## Mapping Your Path: The Power of Self-Assessment

Once you've embraced a growth mindset and are ready to embark on your upskilling journey, the first and perhaps most crucial step is conducting a thorough self-assessment. This process is about taking a clear, honest look at where you stand in your career, identifying any gaps between your current skills and those required to achieve your aspirations.

Self-assessment isn't just a box to tick off; it's a powerful tool for aligning your efforts with your long-term goals. Start by reflecting on both your personal and professional objectives. Ask yourself, "What do I truly want to achieve in my career?" and "How do these goals align with my values?" These questions might seem simple, but they are the foundation of an effective self-assessment. Without a clear understanding of where you want to go, it's challenging to determine the skills you need to get there.

Many of us, particularly women, often struggle to fully acknowledge and showcase our strengths. Identifying our capabilities or recognizing areas for personal growth can be challenging. This can be influenced by societal expectations or even self-imposed doubts. But here's the thing: understanding your current capabilities is essential for moving forward. It's about being real with yourself—acknowledging both your strengths and the areas that could use some polish.

To make this process more concrete, consider using structured self-assessment tools. Skills assessments and competency frameworks can provide a more objective view of where you stand. These tools take the guesswork out of the equation, offering a data-driven approach to evaluate your abilities. This is about gaining a clearer picture of what you excel at and where there's room for improvement.

But don't stop there. Embrace the concept of feedforward alongside traditional feedback. This proactive approach involves actively seeking insights from peers, mentors, and supervisors about how you can improve and grow moving forward. We all have blind spots—areas where we might not realize we're falling short or strengths we're overlooking. By gathering external input, you can gain a more rounded perspective that helps illuminate both areas for improvement and unrecognized strengths.

With the groundwork laid through self-assessment, it's time to move forward by identifying and prioritizing the skill gaps that stand between you and your career aspirations. This is about recognizing what you're missing and strategically planning how to bridge those gaps in a way that aligns with your goals.

Start by benchmarking your skills against industry standards and the requirements of the roles you aspire to. Look at job descriptions, talk to mentors, and research what leaders in your field are focusing on. This benchmarking process will give you a clear picture of where you stand in relation to the expectations of your industry. It's like taking a snapshot of your current skill set and comparing it with where you want to be.

However, not all skill gaps require immediate attention. Some are critical for your career progression, while others can be handled later. Here's where the 80/20 Pareto Principle can be particularly helpful. Focus on the 20% of skills that will deliver 80% of the impact on your career. By prioritizing gaps that are both relevant to your career goals and feasible to address in the short term, you're applying a strategic approach grounded in established personal development models. This ensures you're not overwhelming yourself by trying to fix everything at once, but instead, you're focusing on the areas that will make the most significant difference.

Once you've identified and prioritized your skill gaps, the next step is to develop a strategic learning plan. Setting SMART goals—Specific, Measurable, Achievable, Relevant, and Time-bound—will help you stay on track. These goals should directly address the gaps you've identified, providing a clear roadmap for your learning journey. For example, if you need to improve your data analysis skills to advance in your role, a SMART goal might be to complete a relevant course and apply those skills in a work project within the next six months.

Learning today is more accessible than ever, with a wealth of resources at your fingertips. Online courses, for instance, offer flexibility and accessibility that can fit into even the busiest of schedules. Platforms that provide self-paced courses are particularly beneficial. They allow you to learn at your convenience, whether that's during a lunch break or after the kids are in bed. If you're aiming to step up your game, taking certification courses can really make a difference, especially in fields where the competition is tight. These credentials validate your expertise and help you stand out in the job market.

It's also worth exploring courses specifically designed for women. These courses often focus on areas like leadership skills, negotiation tactics, and strategies for overcoming workplace biases. Tailoring your learning to address these unique challenges can provide you with the tools and confidence needed to excel.

Joining women-specific professional groups has been a cornerstone in my journey and in the journeys of many women I've had the privilege to coach. These groups offer a lifeline of resources, mentorship, and advocacy specifically tailored to the challenges we face as women professionals. I've experienced  how connecting with others who truly understand your struggles—whether it's balancing the demands of work and home or pushing through gender barriers—can be transformative.

For instance, I remember joining a group early in my career that completely shifted my perspective. Engaging with a peer group within this network allowed me to share my experiences and learn from others who had already navigated the challenges I was facing. It's in these settings that you often find innovative solutions to common problems—solutions that are practical because they come from those who've walked a similar path.

Taking on leadership roles within these groups has also been a turning point for many women. Whether you're mentoring other women, pushing for more inclusive policies, or simply setting an example, these leadership roles amplify your influence and impact, both within your industry and beyond. For me, stepping into such roles was a way to give back to the community that had supported me, while also advancing my career.

When it comes to developing a personalized learning strategy, I've found that integrating learning into daily life is crucial, especially when you're juggling multiple responsibilities. I often recommend to the women I work with to find those pockets of time that can be used more effectively—like listening to industry podcasts during commutes or while doing household chores.

Setting realistic and flexible learning goals has been another lesson learned. Life is full of unexpected turns, and it's important to have goals that can bend without breaking. I've seen women, including myself, stay motivated and progress steadily by allowing for flexibility in their learning paths, adapting as needed to keep up with both personal and professional demands.

Finally, I can't stress enough the importance of continuous evaluation and adaptation. Regularly checking in on your progress is about making sure that your learning strategy evolves with your career. This practice has helped me and those I coach to adjust our approaches as our circumstances and goals change, ensuring that we're always moving forward, even when the path isn't a straight line.

## Learning by Doing

When it comes to expanding your skills and career prospects, there's no substitute for hands-on experience. While formal education and courses are important, immersing yourself in real-world challenges through projects, volunteering, or part-time roles can be transformative. These practical learning opportunities offer a chance to apply what you've learned in meaningful ways, all while acquiring new skills that can't always be taught in a classroom.

One avenue that often goes underappreciated is volunteering. I've seen many women professionals who hesitate to volunteer, perhaps thinking it won't contribute directly to their careers. However, volunteering can be a strategic move if approached thoughtfully. Imagine taking on a leadership role in a community project that aligns with your career goals. Suddenly, you're not just giving back; you're also gaining invaluable management experience, learning how to lead a team, and making decisions that carry real consequences.

Skill-based volunteering, or "skillunteering," is another powerful strategy. It's about bringing your professional expertise into a new context—perhaps helping a non-profit with their marketing strategy if you're a marketing professional, or offering financial advice to a start-up if you're in finance. This helps others and allows you to stretch your skills in ways you might not in your day-to-day job. It's an opportunity to experiment, learn, and grow in a supportive environment, where the stakes are different but the learning is just as rich.

Volunteering also opens doors to expanding your professional network. Through these engagements, you meet people from diverse backgrounds, industries, and roles. These new connections can lead to collaborations and opportunities you might never have encountered otherwise. It's a way of broadening your horizons and potentially finding mentors or peers who can support your career journey in unexpected ways.

Moreover, the skills you gain through practical experiences like volunteering or part-time roles are often highly transferable. Whether it's honing your communication skills, improving your ability to work in a team, or sharpening your problem-solving abilities, these are competencies that are valued across industries.

Another valuable approach lies in maximizing the potential of part-time roles and taking on challenging projects within your current job. These opportunities provide a hands-on way to enhance your skills while also making significant strides in your career.

Part-time roles are often seen as supplemental, just a way to earn extra income. However, when chosen strategically, they can offer much more. They can serve as an excellent avenue for acquiring new skills and gaining valuable experience in areas you've identified as gaps in your self-assessment. For example, if you're looking to develop your digital marketing skills, a part-time role at a tech startup could be the perfect setting to learn and apply those skills. Moreover, these roles often offer cross-functional experiences, helping you become more adaptable and broadening your problem-solving abilities.

Taking on challenging projects within your current job can also significantly contribute to your professional growth. It's understandable to feel hesitant about stepping outside your comfort zone—many of us have experienced that. The fear of failure or a lack of confidence can make it tempting to stick with what's familiar. However, seeking out these stretch assignments is a powerful way to develop new skills and build the resilience and confidence needed for long-term career success.

Additionally, working on these projects often involves collaborating with different departments, providing a broader understanding of how various parts of the organization work together. This collaboration enriches your professional skill set and exposes you to diverse perspectives, leading to innovative solutions and a more holistic view of business operations.

It is equally crucial to regularly evaluate your progress in these endeavors. The process of reflection involves more than simply looking back—it's about using those insights to move forward with greater clarity and purpose.

One effective way to reflect is by implementing a structured process like the Gibbs Reflective Cycle, a model developed by Professor Graham Gibbs in 1988. This method guides you through specific stages: describing what happened, acknowledging your feelings, evaluating the experience, analyzing the reasons behind the outcomes, concluding with key takeaways, and finally, planning how to apply these insights in future situations. Engaging in this kind of reflection helps you identify key learning points and equips you with the knowledge to handle similar situations more effectively going forward.

For example, after completing a challenging project, you might take some time to walk through these stages. As you describe the project, a clearer picture of what worked and what didn't begins to emerge. Reflecting on your feelings might reveal underlying motivations or fears that influenced your decisions. Evaluating the outcomes allows you to pinpoint specific successes and areas for improvement. Analyzing why things happened as they did provides insight into the dynamics at play, and by concluding with what you've learned, you'll be better prepared for future projects. Creating an action plan ensures that these lessons are applied moving forward.

On a broader scale, this reflection process can be valuable for career exploration and adaptability. Comparing your current situation with past experiences and future aspirations enhances your understanding of your career trajectory, enabling informed decisions that align with your long-term goals. This practice strengthens career adaptability, making you more flexible and responsive to changes, while contributing to a deeper sense of well-being as you continue to grow in your professional journey.

Personally, incorporating regular reflection into my routine has proven invaluable. It's about understanding the impact of what I'm doing, learning from it, and adjusting my approach for the future. This ongoing process of evaluation and adaptation keeps us progressing, continually growing and succeeding in our careers.

## The Growth Pathway: A Framework for Continuous Learning and Progress

In my journey, I've often encountered women who feel overwhelmed by the sheer volume of skills they believe they need to acquire. They wonder where to start, how to keep going, and whether their efforts are truly paying off. The truth is, learning doesn't have to be daunting. It's about taking small, intentional steps that align with your personal and professional goals. That's why I've developed this growth pathway—a framework designed to help you continuously assess and refine your learning journey.

### Stage 1: Reflection

Begin by documenting your learning objectives and achievements. This is about understanding what these milestones mean for your personal and professional growth. Keep a portfolio of projects and tasks that showcase your new skills and knowledge. This is your evidence, a reminder of how far you've come, and it can be incredibly motivating when you hit those inevitable bumps along the road.

As you progress, take the time to evaluate the impact of what you've learned. How has it changed your job performance? Has it opened up new opportunities or shifted your career direction? Self-assessment tools can be helpful here, but the key is to be honest with yourself. Recognize where you've grown and where there's still room for improvement.

### Stage 2: Review

Next, take a step back and review the learning pathways you've chosen. Were they effective? Did they take you closer to your career goals, or were there detours that didn't quite work out? It's okay if not everything went as planned—this is your chance to learn from those experiences.

Identifying barriers is crucial at this stage. Perhaps time constraints or lack of resources got in the way, or maybe there was a lack of support from your workplace. Document these challenges and think about how you overcame them—or how you might do so in the future. This review process helps you avoid the same pitfalls going forward and makes your learning strategy more resilient.

## Stage 3: Alignment

It's vital that your continuous learning aligns with your long-term career goals. This means regularly checking in with yourself to ensure that the skills you're developing are in line with where you want to go. The industry changes, and so might your aspirations—be flexible and adjust your learning plans accordingly.

Feedback is your ally in this stage. Seek out mentors, peers, and supervisors who can provide insights into your progress. Their perspectives might reveal blind spots you hadn't considered or validate the direction you're heading. Use this feedback to refine your strategies and set new, targeted objectives.

## Stage 4: Implementation

Finally, put those new skills to work. It's one thing to learn; it's another to apply that knowledge in real-world scenarios. Seek out projects or roles that challenge you to use what you've learned. This reinforces your skills and demonstrates your growing competence to those around you.

Keep monitoring your progress. Are you getting closer to your career goals? If not, don't be afraid to tweak your learning plan. Continuous development is about being adaptable and responsive to both your personal growth and the demands of your industry.

This growth pathway is a companion to help guide you through the ups and downs of your learning journey. It's there to remind you that every step, no matter how small, brings you closer to your goals.

## Taking the Lead

As you progress on your growth journey, it's crucial to apply the new skills you've gained where it matters most. The best way to do this is to step up and take initiative with new projects. This is about making a real impact in your team and across your organization.

Start by paying close attention to what's happening around you. Look at the projects your team is working on and think about where things could be better. Maybe there's a process that feels outdated, or a project that could benefit from a fresh approach. This is your chance to use your new skills to fill those gaps. It's about being proactive and spotting opportunities where you can truly make a difference.

But it's also important to ensure that your ideas are beneficial to your team and align with the bigger goals of your organization. When your suggestions help drive the company forward, you're improving your own standing and contributing to something larger. Leadership will notice when you're thinking strategically, with the organization's success in mind.

Once you've identified a project where you can make an impact, it's essential to pitch it effectively. Think about how you'll present your idea—highlight the benefits, anticipate any challenges, and be clear about what's needed to make it happen. This involves demonstrating that you're prepared and thoughtful, qualities that will help you stand out as a leader.

Taking the initiative doesn't stop with your own team. Consider getting involved in projects that span different departments. This is a great way to show that your skills are adaptable and can be applied in various contexts. Plus, working with colleagues from other areas of the organization helps you build a broader network. These relationships can be incredibly valuable, offering support and opening doors as you continue to grow in your career.

As you take on new projects and push the boundaries of what you can achieve, there's another crucial element to focus on: communication. How you articulate your value can make all the difference in how your contributions are perceived and appreciated.

It's not uncommon for many women to feel hesitant about self-promotion. The fear of being seen as boastful can hold you back from sharing your accomplishments. But here's the thing: effectively communicating your achievements is about ensuring that your hard work and contributions are recognized. When you tailor your message to fit your audience, whether it's a technical team or senior leadership, you're showing that you understand the different needs and perspectives within your organization. This ability to connect with a variety of stakeholders is invaluable.

One practical way to enhance your communication is by backing up your claims with data. When you can point to specific results or metrics that demonstrate your impact, it adds weight to your words and shows that you're focused on outcomes. It's about telling your story in a way that's both compelling and credible.

Of course, communication isn't just about talking; it's also about listening. Regularly seek feedback from your manager and peers. Establishing a feedback loop shows that you're committed to growth and open to constructive criticism. But it doesn't stop there—what you do with that feedback matters. By acting on the advice you receive and sharing how it's helped you improve, you demonstrate a proactive approach to personal development.

## Learning to Lead: The Sheryl Sandberg Way

As you start putting these strategies into practice, I want to share the story of a leader I've long admired—Sheryl Sandberg. Her career journey is a powerful example of how embracing continuous learning and upskilling can pave the way to remarkable success, particularly in a challenging and fast-paced industry like tech.

Her journey underscores the transformative power of lifelong learning in reaching the pinnacle of leadership, especially within the high-stakes tech industry.

Sheryl's academic and professional trajectory began at the esteemed halls of Harvard University, where she excelled in economics and honed her leadership skills. Later, her MBA from Harvard Business School further solidified her foundation in analytical and strategic thinking—skills that she carried into her subsequent roles at the World Bank and as the Chief of Staff to the U.S. Secretary of the Treasury. InIn these roles, Sheryl tackled complex global economic scenarios, equipping her for the ever-changing challenges of Silicon Valley.

When Sheryl joined Google, she stepped into a role that was constantly evolving alongside the internet itself. Her leadership in developing Google's advertising strategies showcased her ability to adapt and learn swiftly, ensuring the company's dominance in online sales. But it was at Facebook where her commitment to continuous learning truly came to the fore. As Chief Operating Officer, she cultivated a culture of innovation and openness to learning. Under her guidance, Facebook grew into a global powerhouse, with Sheryl advocating for data-driven strategies and a workplace where learning from failures was not an exception but an expectation.

Sheryl Sandberg is also a huge inspiration to women in leadership. Her passion for continuous learning and self-improvement has really made a difference.In her book *Lean In: Women, Work, and the Will to Lead*, Sandberg highlights the necessity for women to pursue their ambitions with determination, continually learning and adapting to overcome the challenges they face in the workplace. This message has resonated with countless women, inspiring the creation of Lean In Circles—small support groups where women gather to network, share experiences, and build essential skills together.

Sandberg's commitment to personal growth became even more evident after the tragic and unexpected loss of her husband. This profound experience led her to co-author *Option B: Facing Adversity, Building Resilience, and Finding Joy*, a book that offers strategies for conquering life's toughest challenges and reinforces the importance of ongoing personal development.

Reflecting on the inspiring journey of Sheryl Sandberg and the importance of continuous learning in her life, it's clear that the power to shape our own path lies within our hands.

So, as you think about your own journey, I encourage you to take a tangible step forward. It doesn't have to be grand or overwhelming—maybe it's signing up for an online course that piques your interest, attending a seminar that aligns with your career goals, or even joining a professional group that offers new perspectives. The key is to start.

Continuous learning is a personal investment, one that will pay dividends in both your career and personal life. Choose your next learning adventure and see where it takes you. Your growth begins with the decision to keep moving forward.

# CHAPTER 5

# CELEBRATE YOUR WINS: OWNING AND SHARING YOUR ACCOMPLISHMENTS

In a memorable conversation, one of my mentors shared an Oprah Winfrey quote with me that has significantly impacted my career ever since. I've frequently used this powerful quote in my own sessions, as it underscores the importance of recognizing our personal growth and sharing it with others in a meaningful way. Oprah said, "The more you praise and celebrate your life, the more there is in life to celebrate." These words highlight the importance of recognizing every bit of progress and comprehending the significant impact it can have on our lives.

As women professionals, this practice of self-recognition and celebration is crucial. In a workplace where our contributions can often be overlooked, self-promotion becomes a necessity. It's about effectively communicating our achievements and ensuring that our work doesn't go unnoticed. This involves taking ownership of our journey and making sure it's visible to those around us.

Let's tackle a widespread myth about self-promotion right off the bat. It's often misunderstood as merely boasting about our achievements. However, it's actually about thoughtfully showcasing our successes to rightfully earn the recognition we deserve. In doing so, we can break through the gender biases and stereotypes that often limit our opportunities for advancement. When we effectively communicate our accomplishments, we open doors to promotions, raises, and the key projects that propel our careers forward. Without this, our hard work can easily be overshadowed, limiting our growth and the impact we can have within our organizations.

Additionally, it's important to recognize that there's something called the "gender promotion gap" that many women face in the workplace. Research has shown that women are often less likely to speak up about their achievements compared to men, even when their performance is equally strong. This hesitancy can have real consequences—fewer opportunities for advancement, and fewer chances to be recognized for the hard work put in. In many cases, employers rely on self-assessments when making decisions about hiring and promotions. When women downplay their accomplishments, it can lead to missed opportunities.

This gap reflects a broader issue in how organizations operate. Many women tend to underestimate their performance, and this can make them less likely to negotiate for promotions or raises. As a result, gender disparities in the workplace are perpetuated. Changing this dynamic requires a cultural shift, both in encouraging women to confidently share their successes and in ensuring that workplaces value and recognize the diverse contributions that all employees bring to the table.

When women start to openly share their successes, something powerful happens—they inspire others. By communicating what they've achieved, they create a ripple effect, encouraging more women around them to do the same. This builds individual confidence and enables a supportive environment where women's achievements are acknowledged and celebrated. It shows that success is possible, breaking down stereotypes and building a culture where women support each other's growth.

Moreover, when women actively participate in self-promotion, it contributes to greater gender diversity within an organization. Studies have shown that companies with more gender-diverse teams tend to perform better, thanks to the variety of perspectives and leadership styles that women bring. Diverse teams are often more innovative and effective at problem-solving, which can lead to better outcomes for the business as a whole. So, when women step up and share their accomplishments, it's not just about advancing their own careers—it also plays a crucial role in the overall success of the organization.

Let me share a story that showcases the transformative power of self-promotion. I once coached Rachel, a consultant at a prominent financial firm. Despite her considerable skill and dedication, Rachel found herself consistently passed over for promotions and key projects. She believed her work would speak for itself, without needing to broadcast her successes. Unfortunately, this approach meant she often faded into the background while her more vocal colleagues advanced.

Realizing the need for a change in strategy, Rachel began to systematically document her achievements and their direct impact on the firm and its clients. Armed with this compelling evidence, she started actively sharing her successes during team meetings and in performance reviews, highlighting how her efforts contributed directly to the firm's objectives.

But Rachel didn't stop there. She seized every networking opportunity within the firm to engage with senior leaders and peers, openly discussing her projects and their positive outcomes. She also took on a mentorship role, guiding junior colleagues, which showcased her leadership capabilities and expanded her influence within the company.

The results were transformative. Her newfound visibility and the clear demonstration of her value led to her selection to lead a major client project—a breakthrough moment in her career. This high-profile project showcased her talents on a larger stage and solidified her reputation as an indispensable asset to the firm.

Rachel's journey powerfully illustrates the importance of self-promotion in the professional world. Being seen and having your contributions recognized are essential steps for moving up the career ladder.

While Rachel's success story stands out, it's important to acknowledge that not every woman has the same experience. Many women face unique challenges in self-promotion, often starting with internalized barriers that can be hard to overcome.

From my experience coaching emerging professionals to seasoned peers, one significant hurdle I've noticed is a belief deeply ingrained in many women: that quality work alone should garner recognition. This belief often springs from cultural norms that value humility and modesty, especially in women. Yet, in the competitive arenas of modern workplaces, where visibility plays a key role in career advancement, this mindset can be a setback.

Compounding these challenges are societal expectations that women should prioritize being nurturing and selfless over asserting their accomplishments. This clash between expected gender roles and the necessities of professional advancement creates a psychological barrier, making it challenging for many women to step forward and claim the recognition they deserve.

It's striking to realize just how deep the discomfort around self-promotion runs for many women. A survey titled "The Self-Promotion Gap" offers insight into this challenge, having collected data from over 1,000 professional women. It illuminates the significant "self-promotion gap" that exists. This term highlights the disparity between the impressive talents, abilities, and accomplishments that women possess and their reluctance to share these strengths publicly.

According to the survey, more than one-quarter of women—27% to be exact—would actually prefer a visit to the dentist over having to talk about themselves in public. It's a telling statistic that underscores the significant discomfort many women feel when it comes to sharing their accomplishments.

This tendency to make themselves seem less accomplished is particularly concerning when we consider the persistent gender pay gap and the various forms of inequality that women continue to face in the workplace. By hiding their light under a bushel, women limit their own career growth and miss the opportunity to inspire others.

One of the most revealing findings of the study is that 83% of women said they find other women's accomplishments inspiring. This means that when women shy away from sharing their successes, they aren't just holding themselves back—they might also be depriving their peers of motivation and the valuable insights that could help them in their own careers.

So, the question becomes: what if, instead of shying away from self-promotion, we embraced it as a way to lift each other up?

## From the Shadows to the Forefront

To effectively champion self-promotion, we need to start with a fundamental mindset shift—one that centers on regular self-recognition. This goes beyond simply acknowledging your efforts; it's a transformative way to view your contributions and worth in the workplace. This shift is crucial because it lays the groundwork for building the confidence needed to share your achievements openly and authentically.

In the early stages of my career, I struggled immensely with self-promotion. I often downplayed my achievements, convinced that my work would speak for itself. I believed that humility was the right approach and avoided talking about myself, focusing instead on my team's accomplishments. It felt uncomfortable, almost self-serving, to mention my own contributions. As a result, I missed out on promotions and key projects because no one realized I was capable of taking on more. I waited, believing my superiors would notice my hard work, but that never happened.

The turning point came when I saw a male colleague, who did less than half the work I did, getting ahead. He spent time networking, speaking up about his work, and promoting his achievements. He rose through the ranks quickly, while I remained stagnant. That experience made me take a hard look at my approach. I realized that staying quiet was not helping me. I had to make a shift in my mindset—it was okay to talk about my contributions, and I deserved recognition for the work I was doing.

It took time to get comfortable with promoting myself, but once I did, everything changed. I started sharing my accomplishments and the value I brought to the table, and suddenly, people began to notice. My superiors paid attention, and I found myself inspiring other women to do the same. I always encourage women to speak up about their achievements because we've been conditioned to downplay our successes for too long. It's about taking one step at a time, getting comfortable with owning your value, and understanding that it's not boastful—it's essential.

When you begin to recognize your accomplishments, you start to see the true impact of your work. This recognition is the first step toward overcoming internal barriers like self-doubt and fear of judgment, which often hold women back from self-promotion.

Confidence is key here. The more you practice self-recognition, the more natural it becomes to speak about your achievements without hesitation. When you can genuinely and confidently discuss your contributions, it creates a sense of trust and respect among your colleagues and supervisors. This authenticity in communication strengthens professional relationships, paving the way for collaboration and mentorship opportunities that can further your career.

Moreover, embracing self-recognition can act as a catalyst for career advancement. Women who regularly acknowledge their successes are more likely to seek out growth opportunities, whether it's a promotion, a leadership role, or taking on a new project. When you recognize your value, you are better equipped to present it to decision-makers in a way that clearly aligns with the organization's goals, making it more likely that you'll achieve your career objectives.

But this mindset shift does more than just benefit you— it can ripple outward, creating a culture of acknowledgment and appreciation within your organization. This kind of culture boosts employee morale, productivity, and retention, which ultimately benefits the entire organization.

One question I often encounter is, "How do you embrace this journey of self-recognition?" Drawing from my personal playbook, I've found certain strategies particularly effective in ensuring that achievements don't just pass by unnoticed.

First up, develop a personal achievement framework. I've structured my reviews to occur quarterly, which allows me to assess my progress against set goals. During these sessions, I identify key successes and plan how to celebrate them. This method ensures that I don't lose sight of small wins amid daily hustle. It's about taking stock of where you've shined and giving those moments the recognition they deserve.

Then, there's integrating these celebrations into team culture. I encourage teams to hold regular meetings dedicated solely to sharing individual and collective successes. This practice highlights personal achievements and builds a supportive atmosphere that recognizes everyone's contributions.

Crafting a narrative around your achievements can also transform a simple list of accomplishments into a compelling story of your professional growth. I like to connect each success both to personal growth and to how they've propelled the broader goals of the organization. This narrative paints a picture of progression, purpose, and impact.

To really make your success portfolio pop, consider using multimedia elements like videos, presentations, or infographics. These can bring your achievements to life, providing an engaging way to showcase your growth. Whether it's during evaluations or interviews, a dynamic portfolio can make a memorable impact, setting you apart from the crowd.

Another approach that has made a noticeable difference in my self-recognition routine is developing a personalized affirmation program. This is about integrating them into your daily life in ways that resonate with you. For instance, you could set reminders on your phone to take a moment and reflect on your strengths or keep affirmation cards at your desk as a soft nudge to remember what you're capable of.

Another effective method is recording your affirmations and listening to them during your commute. Tailoring these affirmations to areas where you seek growth or confidence ensures that they're not just words, but powerful tools for self-improvement.

Pairing these affirmations with mindfulness practices can elevate their impact. For instance, combining affirmations with a few minutes of meditation or deep breathing exercises can help reduce stress and create a mental space where these positive statements are more likely to take root. This practice reinforces a positive self-perception and helps you approach your day with a clearer, more focused mindset.

Furthermore, I often recommend a crucial approach to my clients: building communities within the organization to celebrate each other's achievements. These communities create a more personal and engaging environment where colleagues can share and recognize contributions. Additionally, we can amplify these achievements beyond the organization by highlighting them on social media platforms like LinkedIn. This approach creates a culture of recognition and positions everyone's successes as a shared victory.

You can also take this a step further by hosting informal recognition events. Whether it's a monthly lunch or a coffee break, these gatherings offer a chance to share and celebrate wins in a relaxed setting. They also provide opportunities for networking and building stronger professional relationships. By creating these moments of visibility, you enhance your own presence and that of your peers, contributing to a culture where everyone's accomplishments are valued.

## Articulating Achievements with Authenticity

When it comes to sharing your achievements, the goal is to find a way that feels authentic—something that resonates with you and others without sounding boastful. This can be tricky, especially for women who may have been conditioned to downplay their successes.

One practical technique I've seen transform how women present their accomplishments involves shifting the focus from personal praise to the tangible benefits their efforts have brought to their teams and organizations. Instead of cushioning your achievements with qualifiers that might diminish their perceived value, try framing them in a straightforward, factual manner. For instance, rather than prefacing your success with, "I don't mean to brag, but...," opt for a clear and direct statement like, "My leadership on the project led to a 20% increase in productivity." This method communicates your role in a positive outcome without implying self-aggrandizement.

Moreover, integrating your accomplishments into the broader goals of your team or organization can be incredibly effective. When you discuss how your actions have advanced or aligned with the company's objectives, your contributions are seen both as personal victories and crucial elements in the collective success. This perspective places your achievements in a context that's relevant to your audience and underscores your strategic commitment to the organization's mission.

As you concentrate on repositioning your achievements and communicating them effectively, it's important to be aware that many women often understate their successes. You might find yourself attributing a job well done to luck or dismissing your hard work by saying, "It was nothing." This habit, while seemingly modest, can actually undermine your value in the eyes of others and lead to missed opportunities for recognition.

One way to overcome this tendency is by embracing a more balanced narrative. It's important to acknowledge your role in your successes while also recognizing the contributions of your team. For example, instead of brushing off a compliment or minimizing your role, you could say, "I played a key role in the project's success, and I'm grateful for the team's support." This statement strikes a balance between confidence and humility, affirming your contributions without appearing boastful.

Another challenge women often face is the "likeability penalty." Self-promotion can sometimes be perceived negatively, particularly when women are assertive about their achievements. This fear of being labeled as too aggressive or ambitious can lead to reluctance in sharing your successes.

To tackle this, focus on building authentic relationships and demonstrating how your achievements benefit others. When you frame your accomplishments in terms of their positive impact on the team or organization, it helps to soften any perceived assertiveness. For example, instead of saying, "I implemented this strategy," try, "By implementing this strategy, I helped the team achieve our quarterly targets, benefiting the entire department." This reframing highlights your role and shows your commitment to the collective success of the team.

To further ensure that your self-promotion is effective and well-received, consider developing a concise personal value proposition. This statement highlights your unique skills and the value you contribute to your role. It's a way of communicating your achievements succinctly and confidently, making sure that others understand your contributions without perceiving them as boastful.

Whenever possible, support your claims with data or specific examples. Quantifying your contributions—such as noting a percentage increase in sales, a project completed ahead of schedule, or a client satisfaction rate—provides concrete evidence of your impact. This approach makes your claims more credible and shifts the focus from self-promotion to factual reporting of your contributions.

It is also important to leverage the power of strategic storytelling. This approach can transform how you share your successes, making them more engaging and impactful. Instead of simply listing your accomplishments, think about them as part of a larger narrative. For instance, when you talk about a project you led, begin by setting the context—what challenges did you face? Then, walk your audience through your process, highlighting the key decisions you made and the skills you employed. Finally, share the outcome and the difference it made, both for you and your team. This method helps your story resonate on a deeper level, making it memorable and relatable.

In addition to framing your achievements as stories, it's essential to convey your genuine passion for your work. Enthusiasm is infectious, and when others see how invested you are in your projects, they're more likely to appreciate your contributions. By sharing your excitement, you draw people in and inspire them with your dedication.

Another effective way to highlight your accomplishments is through what I like to call "stealth-promotion." This involves promoting yourself indirectly by sharing knowledge or best practices with others. Leading a workshop, writing an article, or even participating in a panel discussion are all ways to demonstrate your expertise. By positioning yourself as a resource, you naturally bring attention to your achievements without overtly promoting them, which can feel more comfortable and authentic.

Encouraging a culture of peer recognition is also crucial. When you and your colleagues regularly acknowledge each other's successes, it creates a supportive environment where everyone's contributions are valued. This practice amplifies your achievements and inspires a sense of community and shared success, which can be incredibly motivating.

## Making Your Mark Known

In today's digital age, leveraging platforms like LinkedIn is another important strategy. Many women professionals aren't fully utilizing these tools, which means they're missing out on chances to develop their personal brand. I constantly encourage my peers and clients to actively engage with these platforms. A great way to start is by creating a captivating summary that showcases your career path and the significant impacts you've made. Use concrete examples and metrics to show the value you bring, making your profile stand out to potential employers or collaborators.

Additionally, consider sharing articles or posts that reflect your expertise and experiences. By contributing thought pieces, you position yourself as a leader in your field while subtly showcasing your achievements. And don't underestimate the power of recommendations—having colleagues, supervisors, or clients endorse your skills can add significant credibility to your profile.

One of the most accessible platforms within any organization is the company intranet or other internal communication channels. These tools often provide underutilized opportunities to share your work in a way that reaches a broad audience of colleagues and decision-makers. Consider contributing to internal blogs or newsletters where you can write about the projects you've led. These articles offer a chance to reflect on the challenges you faced, how you tackled them, and the tangible results that followed. By sharing these stories, you highlight your skills and contributions, inspiring others within the organization who might be facing similar challenges.

Another powerful approach is to create a digital portfolio on your company's internal platforms. This portfolio can serve as a comprehensive showcase of your work, including detailed project summaries, key presentations, and any awards or recognition you've received. It's a centralized resource that you can easily share with colleagues and supervisors, making it easier for them to understand and appreciate the scope of your contributions.

Virtual town halls and company-wide meetings also present unique opportunities to spotlight your achievements. These forums are perfect for preparing concise presentations that emphasize your role in successful projects. Use visuals to enhance your message, making it more engaging and memorable for your audience. Speaking in such settings reinforces your expertise and builds your confidence in public communication.

Beyond the internal reach, professional forums and online communities can serve as valuable platforms for showcasing your work to a broader audience. Sharing detailed case studies or project accounts in these spaces allows you to highlight the strategic decisions you made, the challenges you overcame, and the outcomes you achieved. Engaging in Q&A sessions or participating in panel discussions within these communities also positions you as a thought leader, giving you a chance to articulate your achievements and insights in a way that resonates with peers in your industry.

Hosting webinars or virtual workshops can further extend your influence. These sessions provide a platform to discuss your work in depth, sharing not just what you accomplished, but how you did it and what others can learn from your experience. By leading these discussions, you establish yourself as an expert while also creating valuable learning opportunities for others.

The next powerful approach is developing a personal website. Think of it as your digital business card—a hub where all your professional achievements, skills, and contributions are showcased in one place. On this site, you can include a blog where you share insights from your work, a portfolio of your most impactful projects, and testimonials from colleagues or clients who can speak to your strengths. This website becomes a living document of your career, evolving as you do, and providing a go-to resource for anyone wanting to learn more about your professional journey.

Creating video content is another dynamic way to bring your achievements to life. Short video clips or presentations can be more engaging than traditional text-based updates, allowing you to convey your successes with energy and enthusiasm. Whether it's a quick recap of a successful project or a more detailed explanation of a complex challenge you overcame, videos can capture attention and make your message more memorable. Sharing these videos on platforms like LinkedIn or your personal website can significantly enhance your visibility and impact.

This ongoing narrative of your professional life helps others see the full scope of what you bring to the table and positions you as a leader in your field.

## Turning Resistance into Resolve

When it comes to promoting your accomplishments, it's not uncommon for women, especially in male-dominated fields, to encounter resistance or even jealousy. This can come in various forms, from subtle put-downs to more overt challenges to your authority or credibility. Navigating these challenging situations demands a mix of assertiveness, resilience, and well-thought-out support.

One of the most challenging aspects of self-promotion is dealing with macroaggressions—those seemingly small but frequent slights that can chip away at your confidence. It might be a colleague interrupting you in a meeting or someone else taking credit for your idea. These moments can feel frustrating and diminishing, but recognizing them is the first step toward addressing them. When these situations arise, it's important to respond assertively, yet calmly. For instance, if someone interrupts you, you might say, "I'd like to finish my point," firmly but without escalating the tension. This kind of response helps you maintain control of the situation and ensures that your voice is heard.

Building a network of supportive colleagues is another crucial strategy. Cultivating allies who respect and recognize your contributions can make a world of difference. These allies can help amplify your voice in meetings, back you up when your ideas are challenged, and generally provide the support that makes self-promotion feel less daunting. It's also beneficial to engage with mentors who have navigated similar paths. They can offer invaluable advice on how to handle resistance and provide a model for how to advocate for yourself effectively.

Beyond personal strategies, there's also a larger conversation to be had about pushing for changes within your organization. Advocating for diversity, equity, and inclusion initiatives can create a more supportive environment not just for you, but for everyone. Encouraging open dialogue about these issues helps reduce biases and supports a culture where all voices are heard and valued.

## The Road Ahead: Using Achievements as Stepping Stones for Growth

Once you have recognized and celebrated your accomplishments, the following step involves strategically aligning these successes with your career goals and opportunities for future development. This connection is about showing how your accomplishments directly support where you want to go next.

First, it's essential to set clear career goals. These goals should include both short-term objectives, like the next role you're aiming for, and long-term ambitions, such as where you see yourself in five or ten years. When you have a clear vision of your career path, it becomes much easier to identify which of your accomplishments are most relevant to highlight. For instance, if you aspire to move into a leadership position, focus on experiences where you've demonstrated leadership, such as managing a project or mentoring a team.

To keep yourself on track, create a roadmap that outlines the steps you need to take to achieve your goals. This roadmap should include key milestones that align with your accomplishments. For example, if one of your milestones is to develop strong negotiation skills, you might highlight a successful negotiation in your current role as a key accomplishment that brings you closer to your goal.

Another valuable strategy is to engage in scenario planning. This involves thinking through different potential career paths and how your current achievements could support those paths. For instance, consider what might happen if you decide to pivot into a different industry or take on a completely new role. By aligning your accomplishments with various "what-if" scenarios, you can be prepared for a range of opportunities and make informed decisions about how to navigate your career.

## Mapping Success Using the STAR Method

I'd like to share a technique that's really helped me align my achievements with my goals—the STAR method. Although it's often used in interviews, it's also a great way to reflect on your achievements and how they align with where you want to go in your career.

**Situation:** Start by identifying experiences that have shaped your career. Think about the moments where you stepped up, took initiative, or made a difference. These are the situations that reflect not just your past, but also the kind of future you're aiming for. For instance, if you're looking to transition into a leadership role, reflect on a situation where you naturally gravitated towards leading a team or project. It's not just about what you did but about setting the stage for where you're headed. By contextualizing your accomplishments within the framework of your future goals, you're essentially creating a narrative that says, "This is who I am, and this is where I'm going."

**Task**: Once you've set the scene, it's time to zoom in on your specific contributions. What role did you play? What were your responsibilities? Be clear and specific, especially about tasks that align with the skills you need in the next stage of your career. If you're aspiring to be a project manager, focus on how you coordinated efforts, managed timelines, or led a team through a challenging phase. By connecting the dots between what you've done and what you want to do, you're mapping your past while sketching out the future

**Action:** Now that you've set the context and clarified your role, it's time to dive into the actions you took. Think about the specific steps you initiated and how they showcase your strategic thinking and problem-solving abilities. For instance, if you're aiming for a role in strategic planning, highlight moments where you analyzed data, made critical decisions, or led a team through a complex challenge. This is where you get to show how you didn't just follow a plan—you created one. The accomplishments you emphasize should be those that demonstrate the skills you're eager to apply in your next role.

## Result: Quantifying and Reflecting on Outcomes

Next, it's crucial to reflect on the results of your actions. Did your strategic actions lead to a significant increase in efficiency, a boost in revenue, or a measurable improvement in team performance? Highlighting these accomplishments with concrete numbers or metrics shows what you did and how it mattered.

And beyond just the numbers, take a moment to reflect on how these accomplishments have prepared you for your next career step. How have these successes enhanced your skills, built your reputation, or readied you for the challenges ahead? This reflection helps you connect your past achievements with the future roles you're aiming for, making your career trajectory clear both to others and to yourself.

It is important to carry forward the momentum we've built in understanding the power of aligning our accomplishments with our aspirations. But knowledge alone isn't enough. It's time to put these insights into practice, to make recognizing and sharing your achievements a regular part of your professional routine.

The idea of self-promotion might still feel a bit uncomfortable, but think of it as sharing your story—one that deserves to be told. By making it a habit, you gradually shift the narrative, both for yourself and for other women in the workplace who may struggle with the same challenges.

So here's my challenge to you: Start today. Take a moment to reflect on your recent wins, no matter how big or small. Then, find a way to share them—whether it's a casual mention in a meeting, a post on your professional network, or a discussion during your next performance review. And don't stop there. Make it a part of your routine, something you do consistently.

When you do this, you're advocating for your own growth and contributing to a culture where women's achievements are seen, heard, and valued.

# CHAPTER 6

# NEGOTIATE LIKE A PRO: SETTING EXPECTATIONS AND PLANNING YOUR CAREER PATH

In the fast-paced world of automotive engineering, I stumbled upon an inspiring story about my friend Rita from my professional network. For nearly ten years, Rita has been a key player at a well-known car manufacturer. Despite her undeniable success and expertise, she noticed a disheartening trend: her male colleagues were often chosen for high-profile projects before she was, even when her qualifications spoke volumes to her capability.

Facing this familiar obstacle, Rita recognized that advancing in her career required strategic negotiation. She needed to advocate for herself, not just for a promotion, but for the chance to lead a project that could take her career to the next level. In a field where women sometimes find their achievements overshadowed or minimized, Rita knew the importance of coming to the negotiation table prepared.

With careful precision, Rita compiled a dossier of her contributions. She highlighted specific projects where her leadership directly enhanced performance metrics, slashed costs and infused innovative thinking into routine processes. She took it further by aligning her pitch with the company's forward-thinking goals, particularly the electric vehicle initiative she was passionate about leading.

When Rita walked into the meeting with senior management, her energy was palpable. She began with a warm acknowledgment of the company's mission, sharing her deep commitment to its ongoing success. Then, transitioning to her main agenda, she presented a compelling case for why she was the perfect fit to lead the electric vehicle project. Her presentation was backed by solid data and clear examples of her past successes.

She knew she might face some skepticism, perhaps doubts about her handling such a high-stakes initiative. Rita tackled these head-on. With a well-thought-out project plan in hand, she detailed her strategy and discussed her knack for pulling together diverse teams, a crucial element for the success of this ambitious project.

Throughout the negotiation, Rita encountered the kind of subtle biases that many women in her field do. Yet, she didn't falter. Staying confident and focused, she used her thorough preparation to parry each objection with facts and well-reasoned responses. She made it a point to listen actively, showing her colleagues that she valued their input and was addressing their concerns thoughtfully.

A defining moment came when a senior executive expressed concerns about risk management. Rita didn't miss a beat. She outlined her comprehensive risk management strategies with such clarity and assurance that the room's energy shifted from doubt to support.

Her persistence paid off. Rita secured the leadership role on the electric vehicle project, a significant leap forward in her career. This success set a new benchmark within the company.

It opened the door for other women in the company to see what's possible when you stand your ground and negotiate with confidence and clarity.

## The Power of Asking

While Rita's story may sound like a standout success, for many of us, it's far from the norm. Growing up, many of us heard phrases like, "Nice girls don't ask. "These lingering messages contribute to wider inequality in the workplace, where negotiation—or often the absence of it—plays a significant role.

Many women don't receive what they rightfully earn simply because they don't ask. Research underscores this point sharply. For instance, a study by Small, Gelfand, Babcock, and Gettman revealed a telling gap between male and female MBA graduates from Carnegie Mellon. The findings were stark: men negotiated their starting salaries to be 7.6% higher, or almost $4,000 more than their female counterparts. Only 7% of the women had attempted to negotiate their salaries compared to 57% of the men. The difference wasn't in their qualifications, but in their willingness to ask for more.

Researchers have long been curious about why women tend to negotiate less, and the answer isn't as straightforward as a lack of confidence or skill. It has more to do with how women are perceived when they negotiate. Several studies have explored this, looking at how people react to employees who ask for more pay versus those who don't. One key finding is something called the "social cost" of negotiation—the impact on how willing others are to work with that person afterward.

Here's the hard truth: when women negotiate, they often face greater social costs than men. In multiple studies, people were more hesitant to work with women after they had negotiated, whereas men rarely faced the same fallout. Men can certainly push too hard and ruffle feathers, but in most cases, their negotiating doesn't affect their relationships in the same way. For women, though, that cost is very real. It can feel like a double-edged sword—if you negotiate, you risk being seen as too aggressive; if you don't, you miss out on what you deserve.

And it doesn't stop with salary. Negotiation for women in the workplace goes far beyond money. It's also about shaping the kind of career you want, from defining your role to seeking new opportunities that align with your goals. Negotiating can give women a clearer sense of direction, helping to avoid the kind of role ambiguity that often leaves contributions overlooked. By asking for specific responsibilities, leadership in key projects, or expanded roles, women can take control of how their careers evolve and ensure their talents are being recognized where they matter most. Think about the training programs, industry conferences, and certifications that keep you competitive and sharp in your field. Women who proactively negotiate access to these resources align their immediate roles with their broader career ambitions.

Moreover, for women aiming to break through the glass ceiling, negotiation becomes indispensable. This involves laying out your unique contributions and demonstrating readiness for bigger responsibilities. It means negotiating for mentorship, advanced leadership training, and the resources you need to succeed once you step into those new roles.

These conversations are key to paving the way for ascent in traditionally male-dominated industries.

Additionally, steering the direction of your career through negotiation allows you to ensure your current job aligns with your long-term objectives. It entails having strategic discussions with your employer about potential career paths and advocating for roles or projects that offer the right kind of experience and exposure for your future goals.

This proactive approach allows women to be seen for their strengths and ambitions, rather than simply fitting into a predefined mold.

Exploring how negotiation shapes the career paths of women, it's crucial to confront the challenges that might stand in the way of effective negotiation. While the old stereotypes about women's capabilities as leaders are slowly being dismantled, some persistent myths continue to create barriers—especially the notion that women are not as effective at negotiating as men. This stereotype lingers, unsupported by evidence, and it colors the perception of women's negotiation skills.

The obstacles women encounter at the negotiation table are multifaceted. Some of the challenges we initially dissected arise from cultural norms and personal upbringings that can discourage women from advocating assertively for themselves. Others are external, influenced by the attitudes and behaviors of colleagues and superiors. Negotiation inherently involves a degree of conflict, positioning parties on seemingly opposite sides. This setup can be intimidating, and if you view negotiation as a potential threat to workplace relationships, it might lead you to pull back or negotiate with less assertiveness.

Areen Shahbari, who leads a women's leadership program at Harvard, highlights another crucial aspect: women often prioritize maintaining interpersonal relationships over the negotiation itself. This focus can be a double-edged sword, as it might lead to compromises that undervalue their contributions.

Another pervasive challenge I've noticed when interacting with many talented women is that they often underestimate their own professional worth. Without a solid grasp of your own value, setting goals and negotiating effectively for what you deserve can seem daunting. Recognizing and addressing this common pitfall is a critical first step toward becoming more confident and proactive in negotiation scenarios at work.

## Knowing Your Worth

One of the most valuable tools you can have in your professional toolkit is the ability to evaluate yourself—your skills, achievements, and the areas where you want to grow. Knowing your worth in your organization and industry is absolutely crucial for negotiating a better salary or a more exciting position.

In my years of coaching, I've seen time and again how self-evaluation can transform a person's confidence. For women, who often face a "confidence gap" that makes them hesitant to negotiate, this process can provide a much-needed foundation. When you take the time to really assess your contributions, looking at the projects you've led, the impact you've made, and the skills you've developed along the way, you begin to see concrete evidence of your own value. This isn't about inflating your accomplishments—it's about getting a clear view of what you've already done and where you want to go next.

Many of us are well aware of the unconscious biases that still exist in the workplace. Women are often overlooked, or their contributions minimized, because of these ingrained perceptions. But a thorough self-evaluation helps you counteract that. When you have facts—numbers, results, and specific examples of how you've contributed—it's a lot harder for anyone to argue with your worth. And when you approach negotiations with that level of clarity, it shifts the conversation in your favor.

Beyond understanding your current value, self-evaluation is also a great way to align your personal goals with the goals of your organization. What do you want to achieve, and how can that align with what the company needs? When you have a strong sense of this, you're able to take a more strategic approach to your career planning, opening up opportunities to negotiate for roles and projects that challenge you and move you closer toward the career you envision.

If you're feeling a bit daunted by the idea of self-evaluation, you're not alone. It can seem like a big task, but breaking it down into manageable steps can make all the difference. Let me share some practical strategies that have helped many of my clients gain clarity on their professional value.

Starting with a personal SWOT analysis can be incredibly insightful. This method allows you to map out your Strengths, Weaknesses, Opportunities, and Threats. It's a great way to get a bird's-eye view of where you excel and where you might need some improvement. Understanding your own strengths and weaknesses, in conjunction with the opportunities and threats in your environment, lays the groundwork for strategic career planning.

Next, let's talk about the power of data. Leveraging data analytics to review your performance metrics brings an objective edge to your self-assessment. Whether it's the revenue you've generated, projects you've spearheaded, or efficiencies you've introduced, having concrete numbers to back up your contributions can significantly boost your confidence and negotiating power.

Another helpful approach is competency mapping. This involves comparing your skills and competencies against industry standards and organizational expectations. It's about identifying not just where you fit, but also where you stand out. This kind of alignment is crucial for spotting both opportunities for growth and areas where you're already leading the way.

And, don't underestimate the value of feedback. Engaging with mentors and peers to discuss your performance can provide you with insights that you might not have considered. Feedback from those who know your work well validates your self-view and can unveil new areas for development or highlight achievements that you might have taken for granted.

Another effective tool to consider is the use of psychometric and personality assessments. Instruments like the Myers-Briggs Type Indicator (MBTI) or the CliftonStrengths assessment can unlock a deeper understanding of your behavioral traits and inherent strengths. By getting to know your personality type, you can discover how to best leverage your natural tendencies in the workplace. This is about understanding how your unique traits can influence your work relationships and negotiation approach.

Alongside personality assessments, conducting a comparative market analysis is equally crucial. This involves researching current industry trends, salary benchmarks, and role expectations within your field. It's one thing to know your own capabilities, but understanding how they stack up against peers in similar roles provides a critical context. This type of analysis helps you identify where you stand in the market and recognize strategic opportunities for career advancement.

These steps, when taken together, enable you to approach professional negotiations with a solid portfolio of evidence that supports your case. It transforms negotiation from a daunting challenge into an informed discussion about how your skills and contributions uniquely benefit your organization

## Setting Your Sights

Understanding the industry standards for roles and responsibilities is crucial to negotiating effectively in the workplace, especially for advanced positions. This knowledge helps set clear benchmarks for your negotiations, ensuring you're equipped with a broader industry perspective.

An effective strategy that has helped me is to dive into comprehensive industry reports and salary surveys. Resources like Glassdoor, PayScale, and industry-specific publications offer a wealth of data detailing roles, responsibilities, and compensation across different sectors. This information is invaluable, providing a clear picture of what's expected and what's achievable in your field, which can greatly strengthen your position in negotiations.

Another approach I often discuss is the importance of analyzing job descriptions from various companies within your industry. This exercise helps you understand common responsibilities and expectations tied to specific roles. By comparing these descriptions, you gain insights into standard requirements, which can serve as a solid foundation during your negotiation talks.

Additionally, I encourage joining industry-specific professional networks and associations. These groups provide access to exclusive research, reports, and networking opportunities that can be crucial in staying informed. The insights and anecdotes shared by peers in these networks are empowering since they offer real-life examples of negotiation and career advancement.

Once you've gathered the necessary insights into industry standards, the next step is to use that information to set meaningful benchmarks for your negotiations. This is something I always advise the women I work with, as it creates a solid foundation for any conversation about your role, responsibilities, or compensation.

Start by breaking down your current role into specific tasks and responsibilities. Quantifying what you do on a daily basis and comparing it to what's expected across your industry can highlight any gaps or areas where you may be going above and beyond. This quantitative analysis is incredibly helpful in identifying where your role might exceed typical expectations—and that can provide you with a strong basis for asking for more in your negotiations.

Another crucial element is tracking your performance metrics and outcomes. I recommend gathering concrete data that shows how your contributions have positively impacted the organization. Whether it's improving efficiency, completing projects ahead of schedule, or directly contributing to revenue growth, these objective measures carry weight in negotiations. Having hard numbers to back up your claims can really help solidify your case.

If your organization provides access to internal data, use it. Comparing your role, responsibilities, and compensation with those of your peers can be incredibly revealing. If there are discrepancies, this information becomes invaluable in justifying your negotiation points. It's one thing to know the industry standard, but having company-specific data makes your argument even more compelling.

Employing these strategies, you can confidently approach negotiations with a comprehensive understanding of your value and how it compares to industry expectations.

## Stepping Into Negotiation

The next step is to prepare for the actual negotiation. For many women, this is where things get tricky. It's important to recognize that negotiation isn't just a one-time event; it's something you should be prepared to do at critical moments throughout your career—on your way in, as you establish your role, on your way up as you seek advancement, and even on your way out, ensuring favorable terms when you exit a company.

But let's acknowledge the elephant in the room: negotiation can bring up a lot of fear. Many women worry about damaging relationships, encountering backlash, or being seen as difficult. These fears are real, but they can be managed with the right strategies. One powerful way to mitigate these concerns is by approaching negotiation as a collaborative process rather than a confrontation. When you frame the conversation as an opportunity to work together toward a solution, it feels less like a battle and more like problem-solving, which can help reduce the fear of being perceived negatively.

When it comes to overcoming the fear of not being liked, I always remind myself, my peers, and my clients to focus on being respected for your skills and professionalism. Earning respect will take you much further in your career than being liked ever will.

As you step into the negotiation process, another useful tool to keep in mind is positive priming. This may sound simple, but it's incredibly powerful. Before entering any important conversation, especially one like a negotiation that might feel intimidating, it helps to engage in activities that put you in a positive mindset. This could be something as simple as recalling a moment where you felt proud or accomplished or even taking a few minutes to do something that brings you joy. These positive emotions can enhance your creativity and openness, making you more collaborative and calm during the negotiation itself.

Positive priming also has another significant benefit: it boosts your confidence. When you're in a good mental space, you're less likely to feel anxious about negotiating and more likely to approach it with assertiveness and clarity. It's about shifting from a place of stress to a place of empowerment, which can make a real difference when you're sitting across the table and discussing your future.

Of course, no amount of positive thinking can replace the importance of preparation. Successful negotiations always start with being thoroughly prepared. While we've already covered self-evaluation and understanding industry standards, there's another layer to focus on once you're in the negotiation process. You need to think strategically about how you present your case and ensure that the right issues are put forward.

When you're preparing to initiate discussions about your future—whether it's asking for a promotion, a new project, or a stretch assignment—the key is to be ready to clearly articulate the value you bring to the table. This preparation builds your confidence and quiets that inner critic many women face, the one that whispers, "You're not ready yet." By preparing thoroughly, you're not only presenting your skills and accomplishments, but you're also showing that you've thought about how your contributions can directly benefit the organization.

Even if you don't immediately land the opportunity you're aiming for, laying out a strong argument for why you deserve consideration can set things in motion.Sometimes, just opening the door and putting your ambitions on the table is enough to prompt conversations that lead to growth.

When it comes to negotiating in the workplace, many women are naturally inclined toward cooperation and compromise—qualities that can be strengths in a team setting—but in negotiations, they can sometimes lead to giving in too quickly. Whether you're negotiating for a promotion, a raise, more flexible hours, or a new leadership role, it's crucial to approach these conversations with confidence and a clear strategy. One way to do that is by knowing your BATNA—your Best Alternative to a Negotiated Agreement. This isn't just a fallback plan; it's a way of ensuring you don't settle for less than what you deserve.

I often encourage the women I coach to thoroughly assess their options before entering any negotiation. Whether you're asking for more responsibility, better compensation, or a role that aligns more with your long-term career goals, having a strong BATNA means you can enter the discussion knowing you have alternatives. This knowledge gives you the confidence to hold your ground and avoid compromising too quickly just to avoid discomfort.

And here's the important part—consider more than one alternative. Maybe your BATNA is exploring roles at other companies, taking on a different type of project internally, or negotiating a phased increase in your salary. By having multiple options in mind, you increase your flexibility and make it clear that you are coming from a position of strength.

Another essential element in negotiating as a woman in the workplace is understanding the other party's BATNA. If you're asking for a promotion, think about what alternatives your manager has. Could they promote someone else? Hire externally? Assessing the scenario from their perspective can help you anticipate their moves and adjust your strategy accordingly. This can shift the power dynamics in your favor, allowing you to leverage your position more effectively.

A successful strategy for shifting the power dynamic in your favor during negotiations is to frame your request in terms of what the employer needs. Take, for example, a female executive who was offered the role of CEO at a company based in another state. The board initially offered her a one-year contract, but that timeline didn't work for her family—she had a spouse and school-aged children, and a move would require more long-term stability.

Instead of simply rejecting the offer or focusing solely on her personal needs, she reframed the conversation. She presented a detailed five-year turnaround plan that highlighted what the company needed to hit critical targets and grow over the next several years. She made it clear that, to implement this vision, a five-year contract was essential. The board saw that her plan was directly aligned with their goals, and they agreed. In the end, she advanced the company's agenda and secured the long-term stability she needed for her family.

This example reveals the power of positioning your requests in a way that demonstrates how meeting your needs will ultimately benefit the organization. It shows that you're thinking strategically about the company's future, which strengthens your negotiation and makes it easier for the employer to say yes.

Last but not least, it's essential to balance assertiveness with empathy during negotiations. Women should feel confident advocating for their goals—it is your right to stand up for your needs and interests. However, we know that assertiveness can sometimes be misinterpreted, with perceptions of "bossiness" often coming into play.

One way to assert yourself while avoiding these negative stereotypes is by pairing your assertiveness with empathy. When you lead with emotional intelligence and show that you're attuned to the needs of others, you significantly reduce the risk of facing backlash. Women who can blend these natural strengths—assertiveness and empathy—find that they can negotiate effectively without compromising their professional relationships or being perceived negatively.

## From Practice to Payoff

Just like any other skill, becoming effective at negotiation takes practice. One of the best ways to do this is through role-playing scenarios, which allow you to rehearse your approach, build your confidence, and get comfortable with the negotiation process before you step into the real thing.

Let me walk you through a helpful scenario that many women professionals face: negotiating for a salary increase.

*Scenario:* You are a mid-level manager at a tech company due to negotiate a salary increase. You've discovered that your contributions are significantly above average, yet your salary is 15% lower than that of male colleagues in similar roles.

- **Your Role:** The Negotiator (yourself)
- **Partner's Role:** Your Manager

**Objective:** Your goal is to secure a raise that reflects your contributions and aligns your pay with industry standards and internal equity.

## Preparation Steps:

**Gather Data:** Collect information on industry salary standards for your role using platforms like Glassdoor or Payscale. Compile a list of your specific contributions and their impact on the company.

**Plan Your Talking Points:** Prepare to discuss your achievements, focusing on how they align with company goals and contribute to the bottom line.

## Role-Play Execution

### Opening the Conversation:

**You:** "Thank you for meeting with me today. I've been reflecting on my growth and contributions over the past two years and would like to discuss how these align with my compensation."

**Manager Response:** (Your partner acts as the manager) "Of course, I appreciate your hard work. What specifics did you want to discuss?"

### Presenting Your Case

**You:** "Based on my research and understanding of our company standards, I've noticed a discrepancy in my salary compared to industry standards and our internal equity. Here are some key achievements from the last year... (list specific achievements). I believe these contributions justify a review of my compensation to align it more closely with our standards for this role."

**Manager Response:** (Your partner challenges) "While I understand your concerns, we must consider budget constraints and broader team equity."

### Addressing Concerns and Bias

**You:** "I appreciate the budget concerns, and it's essential we also consider fair compensation for proven impact. Could we explore a structured plan where my salary adjustments are aligned with continued performance metrics? This ensures the company maintains equity and rewards results."

## Closing the Negotiation

**You:** "I value my role and am committed to our mutual success. Can we schedule a follow-up to review detailed proposals on how we can address this equitably?"

## Review and Reflect

After the role-play, discuss with your partner what went well, what could be improved, and how different strategies might affect the outcome. This reflection is crucial for applying lessons learned to real-life situations.

Now, let's move into a new situation where you aim to secure a leadership role on a high-profile project. This scenario helps you tackle potential gender biases and showcase your leadership effectively without being perceived as overly aggressive.

## Scenario 2: Project Leadership Opportunity

***Scenario:*** You are vying for a leadership role in a high-profile project within your organization. The decision-maker favors assertive candidates, and you need to demonstrate your leadership capabilities while managing perceptions to avoid any backlash for being t    oo assertive.

## Objective

- Showcase your leadership skills and vision for the project.

- Tackle potential gender biases in leadership perceptions.

## Role-Playing Setup

- **Your Role:** Aspiring Project Leader
- **Partner's Role:** Decision-maker (such as a department head or project sponsor)

## Preparation Steps

1. **Outline Your Vision:** Prepare a detailed vision for the project, including potential challenges you anticipate and your strategies for addressing them.

2. **Gather Endorsements:** Collect testimonials or endorsements from colleagues or cite past project successes to bolster your credibility.

## Role-Play Execution

### Opening the Conversation

**You:** "Thank you for considering me for this opportunity. I'm really excited about the potential of this project and believe it has the capacity to transform our approach to [specific area]."

**Decision-maker Response:** (Your partner acts) "We're looking for someone who can really take charge and drive this project forward. What makes you the right fit?"

### Presenting Your Strategy

**You:** "I've developed a comprehensive plan based on our current goals and my previous experiences. For instance, [describe a key element of your plan]. My approach combines assertiveness with collaboration, ensuring we can achieve prompt results while enhancing team cohesion."

## Handling Bias

**You:** (If questioned about being too aggressive or too soft) "I understand the importance of balance in leadership. My track record shows that I achieve results through teamwork and innovation. For example, [cite a specific past success]. My strategy aligns with our company's goals of fostering innovation while maintaining a supportive team environment."

## Closing the Negotiation

**You:** "I appreciate your feedback and am open to any suggestions that could refine the plan further. My primary goal is to ensure the success of this project and to contribute to our organization's mission. Let's discuss how we can work together to make this project a model of success for our team."

## Review and Reflect

After completing the role-play, take time to discuss with your partner the effectiveness of your approach, particularly how well you managed to assert your leadership without triggering negative biases. This reflection will help you adjust your tactics for real negotiations, enhancing your ability to secure leadership roles while being true to your leadership style.

As you reflect on everything we've discussed, it's helpful to think of your career as a journey made up of ongoing negotiations and thoughtful plans. The tools we've covered— knowing your worth, preparing thoroughly, balancing assertiveness with empathy, and aligning your needs with the company's goals—are there to guide you. But they only work if you put them into practice. Each negotiation is an opportunity to shape your career, step by step, ensuring that you're advocating for yourself in meaningful ways.

I want to leave you with a quote from Linda C. Babcock, who wrote in *Women Don't Ask*: "Women often don't ask for what they want because they don't know that they can." Let that sink in for a moment. You can ask. You can advocate for what you deserve—whether it's a raise, a leadership role, or flexibility in how you work.

So, moving forward, remember that your career is a series of intentional moves. Approach each opportunity with confidence, knowing that every negotiation is a chance to get closer to the career you want.

# CHAPTER 7

# MASTERING THE GAME: TACKLING OFFICE POLITICS WITH SAVVY

When I first started my career, I made a promise to myself to steer clear of office politics. To me, it seemed like a murky world of manipulation and insincerity, far removed from the values of authenticity and transparency I held dear. I believed that success should come from merit alone—hard work, results, and straightforward dealings with colleagues. The idea of engaging in office politics was unappealing as it felt contrary to everything I stood for.

Yet, as my career evolved, especially within male-dominated environments, my perspective began to shift. I realized that office politics wasn't inherently about deceit or manipulation; rather, it was about understanding the complex social dynamics that exist within every organization. In many workplaces, especially those where men predominantly held power, I saw that informal networks and unseen power structures often determined whose ideas were heard and whose projects received the green light.

Deciding to engage with these dynamics marked a significant turning point. I learned that by understanding the office dynamics, I could advocate for my contributions effectively and ensure my voice was heard. This was especially crucial in situations where women's ideas might otherwise be overlooked or undervalued. Far from being a departure from my values, understanding office politics became a way to uphold them. It allowed me to challenge the status quo, push against entrenched gender norms, and assert my presence more firmly in the workplace. It wasn't about playing games—it was about changing the game.

I know I'm not alone in this realization. Many women I've spoken with and worked alongside have shared similar stories of how they, too, resisted office politics at first. But over time, we all came to understand it as a strategic tool, one that can be embraced without compromising our values. A definitive moment for me was reading Bonnie Marcus' *The Politics of Promotion: How High-Achieving Women Get Ahead and Stay Ahead.* Marcus, a successful entrepreneur and thought leader, laid out the importance of office politics for women navigating corporate environments, especially in male-dominated spaces.

That book shifted my perspective even further. Marcus highlighted how ignoring office politics can be risky for women, particularly those with ambitious career goals. It's easy to think that avoiding office politics is taking the high road, but doing so can actually leave you vulnerable. When you don't pay attention to the dynamics around you, especially in competitive environments, you risk being sidelined, no matter how good your work is.

Marcus's own experience highlights just how crucial it is to understand and navigate office politics. Early in her career, she achieved two rapid promotions and believed that the key to success was simply outstanding performance. This belief was challenged when, after eight years at a company and reaching the role of Assistant Vice President, she faced a significant setback.

Marcus was a strong contender for a promotion to Vice President due to her excellent performance. However, despite her achievements, she was overlooked when the time came to fill the VP position. The issue was that she hadn't connected with the underlying dynamics happening within her company. Marcus had focused solely on her external responsibilities and failed to build the necessary internal relationships with influential figures in the corporate office. By not understanding office power dynamics, she remained out of touch with the decision-making processes and the people who had a say in her career progression.

This critical moment in her career highlighted a crucial lesson: success in the corporate world is not just about what you do but also about how you connect and engage with others within your organization. It's about making sure you're connected and proactive in the broader company. Recognizing the power dynamics and building relationships with key stakeholders can be as critical as your job performance. This story is not unique to Marcus; it resonates with many professionals, especially women, who might shy away from office politics due to misconceptions about its nature.

## Why Play the Game?

As my journey—and those of many leaders like Bonnie Marcus—have demonstrated, simply doing your job well isn't enough to advance your career, especially in environments characterized by complex dynamics and entrenched gender biases. To truly make headway, engaging in office politics is crucial.

Initially, my feelings towards office politics were mixed, reflecting a sentiment shared by many of my peers and countless other women. We often dismissed it as unnecessary or even manipulative, saying things like, "I don't have time for that," or "It's just a waste of my time." This perspective was partly due to a misunderstanding of what engaging in office politics actually means and a reaction to the perceived sleight-of-hand often associated with it.

However, these dismissive attitudes overlook a critical aspect of professional environments, particularly in male-dominated fields. The majority of workplace cultures still predominantly favor traditional male styles of leadership, which poses an additional barrier for ambitious women. What we often encounter today is what's known as second-generation gender bias. This type of bias is subtle and insidious because it's woven into the essence of everyday interactions. Unlike overt discrimination, second-generation bias involves cultural assumptions and behavioral patterns that advantage men and create hidden pitfalls for women. This includes a lack of female role models, gendered career paths, and limited access to crucial sponsorship programs and informal networks of power. Moreover, women often face a double bind: assertive behavior that is lauded in men can be perceived negatively when exhibited by women.

Time and again, highly qualified women are passed over for promotions, not because they lack the skills or experience, but because of a system that continues to favor men. Decisions are often made in informal pre-meeting meetings— gatherings where women are frequently excluded. These are the moments that shape outcomes, long before official conversations even begin.

There are also subtle assumptions that create further barriers. Working mothers, for example, are often perceived as unavailable or uninterested in increased responsibility. Men, feeling more comfortable with other men, are more likely to tap their male colleagues for sponsorships or mentoring opportunities that pave the way for promotions. It's no wonder that when confronted with this type of bias, many women feel sidelined, as if they're fighting an invisible battle with no support. The exclusion from power circles is both a symptom of gender bias and a reflection of how hard it is to build the alliances necessary to break through these obstacles.

I often think of the words of Shirley Chisholm, the first Black woman elected to the United States Congress, who famously said, "If they don't give you a seat at the table, bring a folding chair." It's a powerful reminder that women need to create their own opportunities to be heard and seen, even when the system isn't built in their favor.

Recognizing the importance of office politics in this context is crucial. When leveraged strategically, understanding and engaging in office politics can be a transformative tool for women, helping to break down the barriers that hold them back in environments often skewed against them.

## A Mindset Shift

So, how do you begin engaging with office politics in a way that feels authentic and aligned with your values? The first step is to reframe your perception of office politics. I know from my own journey that this shift can be transformative.

Once I started seeing office politics as a means to advance my career without losing my authenticity, everything changed. Instead of viewing it as a necessary evil, I began to approach it with purpose. It entailed making sure my actions were aligned with my career goals and my values. I focused on what mattered most to me—driving impact, building meaningful relationships, and staying true to my professional mission.

This reframing allowed me to engage with office politics in a way that felt right. I realized that I didn't have to play a role or put on a mask. I could engage thoughtfully and still maintain my integrity. And that's where the power lies—knowing that you can journey through these waters without sacrificing who you are.

After you've reframed your mindset, the next step is to become politically savvy. The good news is that political savvy isn't something you're born with; it's a skill you can learn and cultivate. It's about becoming more aware of the environment you're working in, understanding the power dynamics at play, and knowing how to navigate them effectively.

Through my own experiences and the countless women I've worked with, I've come to identify four key pillars of political savvy that make all the difference in the workplace. These pillars serve as the foundation for building your political capital and setting yourself up for success in environments that are often challenging.

## The Essential Pillars of Political Savvy

The first pillar of becoming politically savvy is understanding the unwritten rules that govern your workplace. Every organization has its own set of formal policies, but behind those are the unwritten rules—the subtle, often invisible guidelines that shape behavior, decisions, and outcomes. These unwritten norms dictate who gets listened to, how decisions are really made, and which actions are rewarded or penalized. For women professionals, decoding these rules can be transformative. When you understand how things truly work behind the scenes, you're better equipped to align your actions with the expectations of the organization, positioning yourself strategically to succeed.

This is where cultural acumen comes into play. It's about being sensitive to the unique cultural dynamics of your workplace. Each organization has its own set of values, beliefs, and practices that shape interactions. The way people communicate, collaborate, and make decisions is often influenced by these cultural nuances. By paying attention to these details, women can better navigate the environment, influence outcomes, and build stronger alliances. This doesn't mean changing who you are, but it does mean being aware of how the culture operates and positioning yourself in ways that align with that.

The next pillar is cultivating strategic attention and awareness. I have noticed that politically savvy women possess keen observational skills. They pay close attention to how colleagues interact, noticing the power dynamics and how decisions are made. These observational skills are essential because they allow you to anticipate shifts in influence and power, and adjust your strategy accordingly. The more aware you are of the interpersonal dynamics and how decisions flow through the organization, the more effectively you can position yourself.

Information is power, and gathering it is crucial. Staying informed about what's happening within your organization—whether it's new developments, key projects, or shifts in leadership—gives you the insight needed to make strategic decisions. But it's not just about internal knowledge. Being aware of broader industry trends and the larger business environment also sets you apart. When you're well-informed, you can contribute to conversations with authority, influence key decisions, and demonstrate your value in meaningful ways. This kind of awareness helps you stay ahead of the curve and ready to adapt to any changes in your environment.

The next pillar of being politically savvy is something I often emphasize with my peers and clients: apparent sincerity. This is one of those qualities that can truly shape how you're perceived, particularly as a woman in leadership. Sincerity is about demonstrating authenticity in your actions and words. When your colleagues and superiors see that you're genuine, they're more likely to trust and feel confident in you.

Women, in particular, face unique challenges around perceptions of sincerity. They are often scrutinized more closely than their male counterparts, making it crucial to maintain consistency and integrity in all professional interactions. By being genuine and upfront, women can mitigate biases and reinforce their credibility as leaders. This entails actively shaping how you are seen by colleagues and superiors, ensuring that your true intentions and capabilities are understood and appreciated.

In my own experience, I've seen how being authentic has helped me build stronger professional relationships. It's not about putting on a front, but rather about showing up as your true self, maintaining your integrity, and being transparent in your dealings.

Following apparent sincerity, strategic networking and relationship building form the final pillar of becoming politically savvy. Cultivating a network of supportive relationships is critical to navigating the politics of any workplace. I always encourage women to build connections across various departments and levels. Don't just network vertically with people directly above or below you—spread out across the organization. A diverse network gives you access to valuable information and resources that you wouldn't have otherwise. Plus, it helps you see things from different perspectives, which can be incredibly useful when tackling complex political situations.

But networking isn't a one-time event. It's about forming genuine connections that are mutually supportive. Keep in touch, offer help when you can, and engage regularly. When your relationships are built on trust and mutual respect, they can become an incredible source of social capital. This strategic approach to networking ensures you have the backing needed to face challenges and seize opportunities, making your journey through office politics both successful and fulfilling.

## Mapping the Political Terrain

To make the most of your political savvy, it's important to actively engage with it and map the political terrain of your organization. Understanding how influence operates within your company is crucial, and it starts with recognizing that there's more to an organization than just the formal structure.

Begin by analyzing both the formal and informal structures. The formal organizational chart will give you a basic understanding of the hierarchy—who reports to whom and the official chain of command. But real influence often lies beyond these formal titles. Informal networks, influential individuals who may not hold a high-ranking title but still have the ear of decision-makers, are equally important. It's the people behind the scenes, those who may not be in the spotlight but hold sway in meetings or have strong relationships with upper management that you need to pay attention to. Identifying these key players will give you a clearer sense of where power truly resides.

Equally important is recognizing the role of committees and task forces within your organization. These groups may seem like side projects, but they are often central to decision-making processes. Who is involved in these committees? Who leads special projects? These groups are often where key decisions are made, and understanding their influence can reveal opportunities for you to engage or position yourself strategically.

Another critical aspect of mapping the political terrain is observing communication patterns. Pay attention to how information moves through the organization—who talks to whom, how frequently, and through what channels. Sometimes, the person who holds the most influence isn't the loudest in the room but the one who controls the flow of information. By identifying these gatekeepers, you can better understand how decisions are influenced and how you might position yourself to be in the loop on important matters.

Additionally, recognizing the different communication styles of your colleagues can be equally revealing. Some stakeholders may be direct and forthright, while others may influence more subtly. Tailoring your communication to fit these different styles can help you build stronger relationships and increase your effectiveness in navigating the office dynamics. Understanding these flows and adapting your approach to suit different personalities can make all the difference in your ability to connect and influence.

The next important step in understanding your organization's political landscape is identifying the key players and alliances that shape decisions. Influence mapping is a tool that's been instrumental in my own journey and for many women I've worked with.

Think of influence mapping as a way of seeing beyond titles and job descriptions. It's a way to uncover who really has the power to make things happen in your organization. Early in my career, I assumed the people with the most important titles were the ones driving decisions. But as I learned more, I realized there's often a whole network of relationships beneath the surface—people who might not have the highest-ranking titles but whose influence shapes outcomes in meaningful ways.

Influence mapping provides a clear picture of these networks. By visually mapping who holds influence, who listens to whom, and where real decision-making occurs, you gain a deeper understanding of how your organization operates. This practice is key to developing what I refer to as "connectional intelligence." Connectional intelligence enables women to understand and maneuver through the intricate power structures that dictate the dynamics of their organizations. It's about identifying who is in charge, who influences the influencers, who the connectors are, and how decisions are actually formulated and passed along.

For me, this process opened up new opportunities, not just because I knew who to approach, but because I became more intentional about how I built relationships. This approach helped me stay true to my values while still finding ways to influence and contribute meaningfully.

When I talk to young women professionals, I always stress the importance of influence mapping. It's a powerful tool that allows you to get a clear picture of the political landscape in your workplace. By understanding who truly holds the power and how decisions are made, you can navigate office dynamics with a sense of strategy. This is especially crucial for women aiming to advance their careers. Influence mapping enables you to align yourself with the right people—those who can help you grow and champion your ideas.

What makes influence mapping so effective is that it helps you spot both opportunities and potential threats. By identifying who can be an ally or mentor, and who might present challenges or resistance, you can build relationships that support your career while also preparing for any obstacles that may arise. It's like having a roadmap for who to connect with and how to handle different situations, so you're never caught off guard.

Another key benefit of influence mapping is that it helps increase your visibility and influence within the organization. Once you understand the channels of power and communication, you can tailor your approach to better resonate with key stakeholders. Whether it's the way you present your ideas or the timing of your actions, this awareness allows you to make a bigger impact.

I've often been asked how to get started with influence mapping, so let me walk you through it. First, begin by identifying the key stakeholders in your organization. This includes both people with formal authority, like executives and managers, and those with informal influence. Think about long-tenured employees or charismatic leaders who might not have the highest rank but whose opinions carry weight. It's important to include both internal and external stakeholders who can influence decisions.

Once you've identified these key players, the next step is to analyze the relationships between them. Pay attention to who collaborates frequently, who tends to be at odds, and who acts as a connector between different groups. Understanding these dynamics will help you identify potential allies, build relationships strategically, and be aware of any friction points you may need to navigate.

Once you've identified the key players and mapped out the relationships between them, the next step is to dive deeper and assess the level of influence each stakeholder holds. It's about knowing who has power—it's about understanding what drives them. Take some time to evaluate their interests, motivations, and priorities. What are their goals? What biases might they bring to the table? Understanding these dynamics can help you determine how their interests either align with or conflict with your own career objectives. This deeper insight allows you to anticipate their responses to certain situations, helping you plan your approach accordingly.

Organizations are constantly evolving, so you'll need to regularly update your map as people change roles, new alliances are formed, or shifts in power occur. Keeping this map current ensures that you stay informed and can adapt to any changes in the political landscape.

Finally, once you've mapped out the political terrain, it's time to use that knowledge to your advantage. Leverage the insights you've gained to engage with key stakeholders more effectively. Tailor your communication to align with the interests of the people who matter most. Look for opportunities to collaborate with potential allies and find ways to mitigate any risks posed by adversaries.

Using this map as a guide, you'll be better equipped to tackle the complexities of office politics, making thoughtful, strategic moves that will help you achieve your professional goals.

## Engaging Positively in Office Politics

Engaging positively in office politics can feel like walking a fine line, especially for women who want to maintain their integrity while also advancing their careers. But it's entirely possible to tackle these dynamics thoughtfully and strategically, using approaches that respect others' perspectives and allow you to influence decisions effectively.

One of the key strategies I've seen work time and time again is cultivating strategic relationships. Building bridges across different departments is incredibly valuable. Early in my career, I realized how important it was to connect with people beyond my immediate team. Engaging with colleagues from other parts of the organization provided me with a broader view of the company's goals and challenges. It also made me more visible in the organization. When you're seen as someone who can work across teams, bringing people together, you're positioning yourself as a key player in initiatives that matter. These relationships open doors to opportunities where your influence can be felt in a more significant way.

It's also important to identify and nurture allies—people who share your goals or can help you advance them. In my experience, these relationships grow over time through regular, meaningful interactions. Whether it's casual check-ins or collaborating on projects, these connections can create a network of support that amplifies your influence. Allies are invaluable because they can advocate for your ideas in rooms where you might not always be present, providing critical support when it comes to decision-making.

Another aspect of office politics that I often encourage women to lean into is using soft power and emotional intelligence. Empathetic engagement, for instance, can be transformative. Women often excel in empathy and active listening, which are crucial for building genuine connections. By taking the time to really understand what drives the people around you—whether it's their goals, challenges, or motivations—you can approach situations in a way that resonates with them. This level of understanding inspires trust, and when people trust you, they are far more likely to be open to your ideas.

Collaboration is another powerful tool. Encouraging a culture of collaborative problem-solving not only brings diverse insights to the table but also ensures that everyone feels valued and invested in the outcome. When you involve key stakeholders in the decision-making process, they are more likely to support the solutions that emerge because they've had a hand in shaping them. This is how you can bring people on board, not by pushing your ideas but by making others feel that they are part of the solution.

Engaging positively in office politics also requires enhancing your visibility and advocating for both yourself and others. One key way to do this is through strategic visibility. It's important to look for opportunities to showcase your expertise and make meaningful contributions. I've seen the power of stepping up to lead high-visibility projects, especially those that align with organizational goals. By taking on leadership roles, you're showing your commitment and demonstrating your capability to handle initiatives that matter.

But it's equally important to advocate for yourself. Communicating your achievements is something many women hesitate to do, but it's essential. Regularly sharing your successes in a way that connects them to the broader goals of the organization helps reinforce your value. And while advocating for yourself, don't forget about advocating for others—particularly for your peers, and especially for other women. I've found that when you help lift others up, you create a culture of mutual support. It strengthens your own position and fosters a more empowering environment for everyone involved.

Next, developing a personal influence strategy can be transformative. It starts with making sure that your ideas and initiatives are in line with the company's larger objectives. When what you're working on aligns with the organization's goals, you'll naturally gain more support from decision-makers.

Staying adaptable is another important part of this. Organizations and industries are always evolving, and keeping yourself informed allows you to adjust your strategies to remain relevant. By continuously learning and staying on top of trends, you can add more value to the discussions and decision-making processes, and that positions you as a key player.

Bringing these strategies into your daily work can really help you handle office politics better. They boost your ability to influence decisions and rally support for your ideas, all while staying true to your values and respecting others. In the end, it's about finding ways to move forward while also nurturing a more inclusive and supportive workplace culture.

## Staying True to Your Values

The final and perhaps most vital aspect of tackling office politics is to remain steadfast in your values. It's one thing to engage in office politics strategically, but it's another to ensure that, over time, you don't lose sight of who you are. This is a valid concern, and many women wonder how they can maintain their integrity while still participating in the political dynamics of their workplace. From my own experience, I've found that there are ways to engage ethically and authentically, and these strategies have been instrumental in helping me navigate office politics while holding on to my core values.

The first step is to develop a personal code of ethics. This is your internal compass, guiding you through the sometimes murky waters of workplace dynamics. For me, this meant defining clear boundaries in knowing what I was willing to do and what was simply off-limits. Having these boundaries in place helped me stay grounded, even when faced with challenging situations. This personal code allowed me to make decisions that were consistent with my values, ensuring that I could participate in office politics without feeling like I was compromising who I was.

It's also important to regularly reflect on your actions. This practice has been key for me, especially as workplaces and dynamics change. Taking the time to reassess your decisions, ensuring that they align with your ethical standards, keeps you on course.

Another important aspect of staying true to your values is building a diverse support network. I've found that surrounding yourself with a range of voices—people who can advocate for you, offer support, and provide honest feedback—creates a scaffolding of trust and accountability. In my own journey, having "truth tellers" who were unafraid to give me constructive criticism helped me stay grounded and avoid potential ethical missteps.

It is important to remember that real influence grows from genuine interactions and meaningful contributions. I always encourage women to use their natural strengths—empathy, active listening, and connection-building—to create authentic relationships. These qualities not only help you build influence but also ensure that your influence is grounded in who you truly are. When your actions align with your values, your leadership feels natural, and those around you are more likely to respect and trust your intentions.

In my own experience, one of the most powerful ways to use influence is by promoting a culture of inclusivity. I often stress to my peers the importance of using their positions to advocate for diversity and equity within their organizations. When you champion inclusive practices, you're contributing to a broader ethical mission. Aligning your influence with these greater goals makes your political engagement more meaningful and reinforces your personal integrity. It's a way of ensuring that your influence creates positive change both for you and those around you as well.

Now, alongside embracing influence with authenticity, there's also the importance of transparency and tact when navigating corporate culture. Transparent communication is one of the most valuable tools in building trust. When you share your intentions openly and clearly explain the reasoning behind your actions, it reduces misunderstandings and helps people align with your goals. This is especially important when you're in a position where your decisions impact others. Proactively sharing information—keeping your team in the loop about organizational changes or key decisions—ensures that everyone feels included and reduces the potential for political misunderstandings.

At the same time, tactful engagement is key. Understanding the corporate culture, respecting it, but still finding ways to maintain your authenticity, is a balancing act. This means adapting your communication style when necessary but without losing sight of who you are. It also means navigating conflicts with diplomacy. I've found that addressing conflicts directly, but with a focus on solutions rather than assigning blame, helps to preserve relationships and reinforces a culture of respect. It's all about finding that delicate balance between standing firm in your values while engaging with others in a way that fosters collaboration and mutual respect.

Staying informed and adaptable is the final piece of the puzzle when it comes to engaging in office politics ethically and effectively. It's crucial to regularly update your knowledge of industry trends, organizational shifts, and changes within your professional environment. This constant learning keeps you ahead of the curve and ensures that your strategies remain relevant, allowing you to tackle office politics with both integrity and success.

When women professionals adopt these strategies, they engage in office politics as a constructive and ethical process. This approach enhances their influence and contributes to a more inclusive, transparent, and ethical workplace. Over time, this kind of engagement can shift workplace dynamics beneficially, creating a culture where values and professional success are intertwined.

With this understanding of office politics, it's time to see it as an essential skill rather than a dark art. Engage with it as you would with any other professional skill—by learning, adapting, and applying it strategically. So, step up and engage. Use what you've learned to navigate your workplace dynamics effectively. This is how you turn potential obstacles into stepping stones for your career advancement. It's your turn to play the game smartly, keeping your integrity intact while you do it.

# CHAPTER 8

# LET'S GET VISIBLE: BUILDING AND LEVERAGING YOUR NETWORK

I want to be upfront as we continue along this path of growth and self-empowerment—what lies ahead will demand more from you than ever before. It's a road that asks for courage, resilience, and the willingness to show up fully, but it's also a journey that will lead to immense fulfillment and growth. I'm reminded of something Brené Brown once said, *"Courage starts with showing up and letting ourselves be seen."* These words carry a weight of truth because they speak to a deeper need—to step forward and allow ourselves to take up space, to be recognized for who we are and what we bring.

"Letting ourselves be seen." It sounds simple, but there's real courage in that. It's something I've found myself going back to, both in my own experiences and in the work I do with the many talented women I've had the honor of coaching. There's power in visibility, and yet, for so many women, there's also hesitation.

In the professional world, staying visible is key to landing important assignments, building valuable relationships, and getting your contributions recognized. When you're visible, you open doors and highlight the unique value you bring to the table.

But here's the catch, and it's one that women know all too well. Research shows that having more women in an organization doesn't automatically translate into reduced bias or equal opportunities. That's because biases are often embedded in the very fabric of an organization—its structures, its practices, and its culture. These systems tend to favor men, making it harder for women to be seen for their full contributions. Often, women are encouraged to downplay their achievements, and when they do assert their authority, they can face pushback. All of this directly affects their visibility, making it even more essential to be seen to challenge these norms and push for a more inclusive and equitable workplace.

But the paradox here is real. When women try to increase their visibility, they can face criticism for stepping outside traditional gender expectations. It's a delicate balance. Women are often caught between wanting to be visible and fearing the backlash that might come with it. And so, many choose to stay in the background, keeping a lower profile to avoid potential conflict.

This is referred to as intentional invisibility. In my career, I've seen countless examples of intentional invisibility. It's a concept that many women, including myself, have experienced at some point. While intentional invisibility might offer short-term comfort, it often limits long-term growth and opportunities. Staying in the background may feel safer, but over time, it prevents us from being recognized for the value we bring. On the other hand, embracing visibility can challenge these internalized beliefs and build confidence in our abilities. Being visible allows us to actively demonstrate our skills and contributions, ensuring they're seen and appreciated.

When women choose to step into the spotlight, they gain recognition for their work and also begin to break down the barriers that keep leadership roles predominantly male.

Visibility creates space to showcase what we're capable of, helping to secure influential assignments and build the relationships necessary for career progression. It becomes a tool for challenging the deeply ingrained gender biases that still exist in many workplaces.

For many women in leadership, networking has proven to be an indispensable strategy. Recent findings from a survey conducted by Chief in collaboration with Morning Consult in July 2023 underscore this point. The survey, which included 751 women at management level and above across the U.S., revealed that networking is crucial for reaching significant career milestones. Whether it's securing a board seat, breaking into the C-suite, or stepping into roles with better compensation, over 80% of respondents acknowledged the role of networking in these achievements.

Moreover, the benefits of networking extend beyond individual accomplishments. By choosing visibility, women are creating a cultural shift within their organizations. When women leaders are visible, they challenge traditional norms and demonstrate that leadership doesn't have to look one way. This helps inspire a more inclusive environment, where diverse leadership styles are embraced and valued. Younger women see these visible leaders as proof that leadership is within reach, regardless of gender.

Reflecting on networking's impact on professional visibility brings to mind a personal story about Meera, a marketing professional from Mumbai. When I first met her at a networking event, she shared how her journey unfolded in a mid-sized advertising agency. Despite being highly skilled and dedicated, Meera felt stuck. Her efforts weren't translating into the promotions she deserved. It wasn't about a lack of competence; the marketing industry, like many others, was still slow in offering leadership roles to women. Meera saw this firsthand as her male colleagues advanced, often thanks to the relationships they cultivated, not necessarily their performance.

Meera realized that she had to make a shift. She needed to be more than just good at her job; she had to be seen. The idea of stepping into the spotlight wasn't easy for her. It felt uncomfortable at first, like she was stepping into unfamiliar territory. Internally, Meera wrestled with imposter syndrome. She frequently doubted her abilities, second-guessing whether she truly belonged in the rooms with industry leaders. This hesitation often kept her from speaking up at events or reaching out to those who could offer guidance.

Recognizing that her self-doubt was holding her back, Meera made a conscious effort to acknowledge her accomplishments, however small they might seem. She leaned on trusted colleagues for feedback, which helped her see her strengths from another perspective. Slowly, her confidence began to grow. She set clear goals for networking and, more importantly, treated these goals like essential tasks in her daily routine.

She began attending marketing conferences and seminars, making a point to introduce herself to speakers and panelists. She didn't just attend passively; she asked thoughtful questions and shared her perspectives, ensuring that her presence was known. At the same time, she realized the growing importance of digital spaces and made sure her LinkedIn profile reflected her expertise. She started participating in online discussions, sharing her insights on marketing trends and engaging with posts from industry leaders.

Over time, this proactive approach helped Meera build a strong network of mentors and sponsors. These individuals offered her guidance and became advocates for her within their networks. This advocacy, in turn, helped her gain the visibility she needed among key decision-makers.

As Meera's network grew, so did the range of opportunities that came her way. She began receiving invitations to speak at various industry events and contribute to well-known marketing publications. Each opportunity amplified her visibility and solidified her reputation as a thought leader in her field. What had started as small, deliberate steps in building connections was now opening doors she hadn't imagined before.

It was during one of these conferences that Meera caught the attention of a senior executive from a leading marketing firm. Her insightful comments and the confidence she showed in engaging with other industry professionals made a lasting impression. After a few conversations, this executive extended her an offer for a leadership role in his company, which provided her with more responsibilities and a voice in shaping key strategic decisions.

Meera's story is an example of how, despite the real challenges women face in professional environments, taking deliberate steps to be more visible and build meaningful connections can lead to significant career advancement.

## Overcoming Barriers

The highs and lows of networking can feel overwhelming, but it's important to remember that the lows are where we do the most growth. This is where we learn to confront what holds us back and develop strategies that advance our careers and build our confidence. One of the first barriers many women encounter is impostor syndrome—a pervasive feeling of inadequacy that persists despite clear evidence of success. Research on this phenomenon, first identified by psychologists Pauline Rose Clance and Suzanne Imes, reveals that societal stereotypes and personal experiences often fuel these feelings among high-achieving women, causing them to doubt their intelligence and accomplishments even as they excel. Harvard Business Review's 2022 article, *"You're Not an Imposter. You're Actually Pretty Amazing,"* emphasizes that many individuals, especially women, struggle with these beliefs, but offers practical, research-backed strategies to combat them, like maintaining a positive mindset and celebrating personal achievements.

A KPMG study underscores the prevalence of this challenge, showing that 75% of female executives have experienced impostor syndrome, which can hinder confidence and affect professional interactions. If you've ever caught yourself thinking, "I don't belong here" or fearing that your achievements might be dismissed as mere luck, you're far from alone. Recognizing these thoughts is the first step. By acknowledging impostor syndrome for what it is—an unfounded belief—you can begin to counter it with the reality of your hard-earned accomplishments.

Another trap many women fall into is believing that a large network is the ultimate goal. It's easy to think that the more contacts you have, the more opportunities will come your way. While having a wide network can be helpful, it's the depth of these connections that truly matters. Meaningful relationships, built on trust and shared values, offer far more support and opportunity than a long list of acquaintances. It's about cultivating a network that understands your goals and advocates for you when opportunities arise.

Based on my observations, another common challenge for women in networking is the lack of access to informal networks where crucial conversations and opportunities often unfold. These networks, which sometimes operate under "boys' club" dynamics, can create a sense of isolation for women, shutting them out from the flow of vital information and connections. When informal spaces are dominated by these dynamics, women are often left with fewer chances to gain insights about upcoming opportunities or strategic moves within their industries.

From what I've noticed, societal expectations and ingrained biases further complicate the networking efforts of many women. The pressure to balance professional responsibilities with personal ones, coupled with a reluctance to navigate male-dominated spaces, can make it difficult to approach networking confidently.

The subsequent roadblock is the tendency for women to underestimate the power of networking in comparison to their qualifications. There's often a belief that simply meeting job criteria or being highly qualified is enough to advance. While skills and experience are critical, networking can serve as a powerful bridge between qualifications and opportunity.

I've also seen that it's essential for women to seek out networks and events specifically designed to support their growth. These spaces offer community, mentorship, and shared experiences. Being part of these circles can open doors to resources and opportunities that might have seemed out of reach in less inclusive environments. Additionally, women benefit from the solidarity and encouragement that come from connecting with others who have faced similar challenges.

## The Connection Catalyst Framework

In order to overcome these barriers, leverage the positives, and effectively lay the groundwork for building a solid support structure, your network, a strategic approach is essential. But how do you start building this network in a way that feels authentic and purposeful?

I've found that networking is most effective when it's grounded in clear intent. This is what led me to develop a practical approach that I call the Connection Catalyst Framework. It's something I've used myself and have seen work for other women.

The first step in this framework is all about creating connections that align with your career aspirations. To do that, you need to get clear on why you're networking in the first place. A lot of women I've worked with initially approached networking as something they had to do, not something they wanted to do. It was just another box to check. But once they stopped treating it like a random task and began to see it as a tool that could bring them closer to their personal goals, everything changed. They stopped feeling overwhelmed and instead started having conversations that mattered.

I remember a peer telling me how defining her networking purpose shifted her entire approach. She was no longer simply showing up at events or reaching out to people for the sake of it. She knew what she was aiming for, whether that was mentorship, job opportunities, or insights into a new industry, and that clarity gave her the confidence to engage in a way that felt real and meaningful.

After defining your purpose, the next step is to take a closer look at your current network by conducting a network audit. This step often reveals valuable insights. Many women I've worked with are surprised by the untapped potential in their existing relationships and the areas where they need to build new connections.

It's about identifying who can support your current goals and noticing where you need to grow. You might find that while you have strong relationships with peers, you could benefit from connecting with people in leadership roles or different industries. This audit helps you understand what's missing and where to focus your efforts to advance.

Once you've assessed your network, it's important to connect with women-focused communities. These networks offer a specific kind of support that many women find invaluable. In my experience, joining these groups can provide more than advice or opportunities. They create a sense of belonging and shared understanding that's crucial for tackling professional challenges.

Women-focused networks are places where you can find mentorship, share experiences, and support each other. Being part of these communities empowers you to grow while helping others do the same. It's a powerful way to strengthen your network and gain the encouragement needed to overcome obstacles in male-dominated spaces.

It is equally important to emphasize genuine engagement. This is where the real magic happens. Authenticity, I believe, is at the heart of building lasting, meaningful relationships.

Relationships built on authenticity tend to be more resilient and fulfilling in the long run. When you show up as your true self, it invites the same in return, allowing for mutual respect and understanding to flourish. In a professional world where women can sometimes feel the pressure to overperform or adopt certain personas, staying authentic helps dismantle stereotypes and build trust.

A crucial aspect of this framework is using online platforms in a strategic way. Platforms like LinkedIn provide immense opportunities to widen your professional circle beyond your immediate environment. The online space has opened doors for me in ways I hadn't imagined, allowing me to connect with industry leaders and professionals across the globe. But it requires a strategic approach.

It's important to present a profile that truly reflects your expertise and professional journey. Sharing insights, engaging in discussions, and participating in industry-specific groups creates a sense of visibility and relevance. This presence highlights your value and brings new opportunities directly to you, from collaborations to mentorships.

By combining authenticity with a strategic online presence, you're setting yourself up for a network that works for you in a real and lasting way.

The final part of the Connection Catalyst Framework focuses on building a Personal Advisory Board, a group of trusted individuals who can provide guidance and support. This board should be made up of mentors, peers, and advisors who understand the challenges you face and offer different perspectives based on their experiences.

Over time, I've seen the benefit of having this type of board in place. These advisors become an important part of your journey, offering the advice and encouragement you need to stay on track.

## The Personal Advisory Board

Creating a Personal Advisory Board (PAB) has been one of the most impactful strategies I've seen women professionals use to advance their careers. It's a powerful, personal tool for building a circle of trusted advisors who help guide your career decisions.

The idea behind a Personal Advisory Board is simple: it's about surrounding yourself with a diverse group of people who can offer honest advice, different perspectives, and encouragement when you need it. These are individuals you trust, who understand your ambitions, and who can give you feedback that pushes you forward. They help you see opportunities you might have missed and point out blind spots that could hold you back.

This kind of support becomes especially valuable in environments where women often face unique challenges. Having a variety of viewpoints from people who come from different industries or backgrounds can give you the insights you need to tackle complicated situations. Whether you're facing difficult negotiations, feeling uncertain about a career move, or trying to balance personal and professional life, this board becomes a personal sounding board that keeps you grounded and focused.

When we look closely at the components of a Personal Advisory Board, each role plays a crucial part in shaping a woman's professional journey. Let's start with the Personal Guides. These are the people who may not even be directly involved in your daily life, but their achievements and paths serve as a source of inspiration. They might be former mentors, leaders in your field, or even historical figures who have broken barriers. For women, especially in fields where representation in leadership is limited, having personal guides is a way to visualize what success looks like. It's about knowing that others have achieved what you aspire to, and that's an invaluable motivator. These guides help you create a mental roadmap, a way to see where you're going even if you haven't reached that level yet.

Next, we have the Personal Advisors, those trusted individuals who offer emotional support. This group often includes close friends or family members, people you can turn to when things get tough. We all know how important it is to have someone who believes in us when we're feeling uncertain or overwhelmed, and for women balancing both professional and personal responsibilities, this emotional support is crucial. It's the personal advisors who remind you of your strengths when you're doubting yourself, who give you the confidence to keep pushing forward even when the path feels challenging.

The next crucial members of your Personal Advisory Board are the Full-Service Mentors. These individuals are deeply embedded in your field and offer far-reaching guidance on both your professional and personal development. Think of them as your go-to experts for everything from skill enhancement to career strategies. They help you refine your craft, offering feedback that pushes you to grow. But beyond that, they are also there to help you tackle the broader aspects of your industry, offering invaluable insights that help you understand how to position yourself for success.

For many women, facing biases that question their competence or leadership potential is an all-too-familiar challenge. Full-service mentors step in to help you build the skills and leadership qualities that reinforce your professional credibility. Their guidance becomes a touchstone for making strategic career moves, setting you up to break through barriers that may have previously seemed insurmountable.

Equally important are Career Advisors, typically colleagues or supervisors who have a closer connection to your day-to-day work. They provide you with practical, real-time advice on how to improve job performance and how to handle transitions within your organization. While Full-Service Mentors might focus on broader career strategies, Career Advisors are your in-the-moment guides, helping you identify strengths and areas for improvement that directly impact your current role.

Next on your Personal Advisory Board are Career Guides, individuals who offer focused support during key career events or decisions. Their role is particularly valuable when you're tackling career transitions, such as layoffs, considering a new position, or even making a significant career pivot. Drawing from their own experiences or deep industry knowledge, they help you make informed decisions at critical moments.

For women, unexpected career shifts can present unique challenges, often requiring quick decision-making that may not always come naturally, especially when facing uncertainty. This is where Career Guides step in, providing timely, situational advice. They help clarify your options, offering targeted guidance that helps you move forward with confidence when you're standing at a professional crossroads.

Equally important are Role Models. These are the people whose success stories inspire you, individuals who've achieved what you may be striving for. For many women, the absence of visible female leaders can fuel self-doubt, making it difficult to see a clear path forward. Role models break down that barrier. They show that there are diverse ways to succeed, validating non-traditional career paths and reassuring you that leadership doesn't have to look one way. By witnessing their journey, you're reminded that your goals are within reach and that your own path, no matter how unique, is just as valid and attainable.

## Mapping Your Path to Power

Mapping out your network helps you see where you are now and where you need to go. It's a strategic process, one that ensures you're making the most of the connections you have, while also identifying the gaps you need to fill to keep moving forward. This kind of intentional networking can make all the difference, especially for women in professional settings where access and visibility are often challenges.

This begins with conducting a network audit. This is about taking stock of who's already in your corner. It might seem straightforward to list out your contacts, but it's important to go a little deeper. Think of everyone in your network and categorize them. Are they colleagues, mentors, industry peers, or perhaps even former supervisors? What roles do they play in your professional life? This process will allow you to see the breadth and depth of your connections.

In my experience, many women find that their networks are either too narrow—focused on one small group—or too broad without a real strategy behind them. Conducting an audit can help fix this by giving you a clear picture of your network's strengths and weaknesses. It allows you to evaluate whether these connections are aligned with your goals or if you need to reach out to new circles.

One practical way to approach this is by using visual tools like mind maps or digital platforms that allow you to map out your network visually. When you see everything laid out, it's easier to recognize where your strongest connections lie and where you might need more depth or diversity.

The next part of this strategy is identifying key influencers within your network. These are the people who have the power to open doors, offer new opportunities, and advocate on your behalf. Key influencers are often those with leadership roles, but they can also be individuals with deep industry knowledge or extensive connections that could benefit you.

A simple starting point is looking at your network map and identifying individuals who stand out in terms of their influence. Maybe they're well-connected within the organization, or they've carved out a niche in an area you want to explore. Reach out to them with purpose, whether it's through a request for a quick coffee chat, an informational interview, or even mentorship.

Now that you've begun identifying key influencers in your network, the next step is to spot gaps and opportunities. This is where you start recognizing the areas where your current network doesn't fully support your career aspirations or lacks the diversity of thought and experience you need to grow. Maybe you're aiming for a leadership position in a new industry, but your network doesn't include anyone in that space. Or perhaps your current connections are too similar to your own background, and you're missing out on broader perspectives that could challenge and enrich your thinking.

A practical way to approach this is to compare your network with where you want to be in your career. If your goal is to move into a leadership role within the tech industry, for example, you'll need connections who are already in tech leadership circles. It's important to take steps to connect with these individuals, whether by attending industry-specific events, joining online forums, or reaching out to professional groups. The idea is to bridge those gaps and build relationships that help you reach your specific goals.

And this is where your Personal Advisory Board (PAB) becomes even more valuable. They can provide insights you may not have considered. With their varied backgrounds and experiences, they might point out gaps in your network that you haven't noticed, or opportunities that you've overlooked. This kind of feedback is crucial in ensuring that your network remains dynamic and aligned with your career objectives.

When mapping your network, regularly discuss your progress with your PAB. They can help you refine your strategy, offering suggestions for where to seek out new connections or how to better leverage existing ones. Their outside perspective can help you avoid blind spots and make sure your network is constantly evolving to meet your needs.

## Power Ties

As you start thinking about the connections you've built, it's important to go beyond just knowing people. What truly matters is how you keep those relationships alive and meaningful over time. That's where being thoughtful about how you engage with different layers of your network really comes into play.

At the heart of any strong network is the core—a group of individuals with whom you already have established, trusted relationships. This core group could include mentors, close colleagues, or people who have been long-term collaborators. These are the people who consistently offer advice, support, and advocacy, making them an essential part of your professional growth. But the key to maintaining this core is through regular, intentional interaction.

Imagine it as maintaining a friendship—you wouldn't only reach out to a close friend when you needed something. It's the same with your core network. Regular check-ins, whether through scheduled calls or in-person meetings, allow you to discuss your career progress, share goals, and address challenges. For women, especially in male-dominated fields, this consistent support helps counter the isolation that often creeps in. These conversations are valuable opportunities to exchange ideas, seek guidance, and gather insights.

Another strategy that can deepen these relationships is collaboration. When you work on joint projects or initiatives with people in your core network, you create shared successes. This strengthens your bond and allows you to showcase your skills and leadership in action. By proposing projects that align with both your goals and theirs, you can create a win-win scenario that boosts your visibility and builds trust.

Your core network also acts as your gateway to valuable industry intelligence. Often, critical information—whether it's industry trends or organizational shifts—is passed through informal channels. Women might not always have access to these networks, making it crucial to leverage the people you trust to fill in the gaps. During these regular interactions, ask about developments in the industry or insights into changes within your organization. These conversations can provide you with a competitive edge, helping you prepare for career transitions or new opportunities.

And finally, don't hesitate to ask your core network to advocate for you. Advocacy can be a game-changer in professional growth, yet many women struggle to find sponsors who actively promote them for opportunities. By maintaining strong, positive relationships and sharing your accomplishments openly, you make it easier for these contacts to speak up for you when needed.

The beauty of these core relationships is that they last—if you nurture them. Celebrating milestones, sharing personal achievements, and adapting to each person's preferred way of staying in touch ensures that these connections stay strong throughout your career. It's about keeping your core network engaged and genuinely invested in your success, while also offering your own support in return.

Once you've strengthened your core network, it's time to expand your reach. Your secondary network, consisting of acquaintances, industry peers, and professionals you've met through various events or platforms, holds untapped potential.

Engaging with this secondary network is about stepping out of your comfort zone. It involves being more active in industry discussions, showing up at events, and sparking conversations. This helps you stay visible and relevant in your field, something that's especially important when it's easy to be overlooked.

Attending targeted networking events, like conferences or webinars, can be a great way to reconnect with old contacts and meet new ones. Approaching these events with an open mindset can lead to collaborations or projects you wouldn't have considered before

You might also consider establishing yourself as a thought leader. Whether through writing articles, giving presentations, or sharing posts on social media, consistently putting your expertise out there attracts others who share your interests. These engagements can spark meaningful relationships and collaborations that might not have happened otherwise.

With your core and secondary networks strengthened, your peripheral network comes into play. This includes distant connections or those outside your usual industry, which can be a goldmine of fresh opportunities and perspectives. Here, you can explore new ideas and even consider career shifts that may not have seemed possible within your current circle.

One of the most effective ways to tap into this broader network is by conducting informational interviews. These are informal, relaxed conversations that give you a chance to learn directly from people who have experience in areas you're curious about. Whether you're exploring a new industry or trying to understand different roles, these conversations are invaluable. They allow you to gather insights without the pressure of job-seeking, and they can often lead to new opportunities down the line. The key is to approach these discussions with genuine interest and respect for the other person's time.

Another powerful strategy for engaging with your peripheral network is joining cross-industry groups. These platforms bring together professionals from diverse fields and open up space for collaboration across different sectors. For women looking to break into male-dominated industries or make bold career pivots, these groups are essential. They offer a mix of innovative ideas and fresh perspectives that can help you stay adaptable and creative.

## Ursula Burns' Journey to the C-Suite

It's only natural to think about the journey of a woman who climbed the corporate ladder and became an inspiring role model by tapping into the power of networking. Ursula Burns, the former CEO of Xerox, is one such figure whose career serves as a blueprint for how networking, mentorship, and strategic alliances can lead to incredible success.

Ursula Burns' story is one of resilience, strategy, and bold moves. She started as a summer intern at Xerox in 1980, and over time, she broke through layers of racial and gender biases to become the first African American woman to lead a Fortune 500 company. Her success was due to hard work and the formation of meaningful connections, having the right mentors, and being recognized for her potential in a system where visibility wasn't easily granted.

One of the key turning points in Ursula's career was the ally she found in Paul Allaire, the CEO of Xerox at the time. Allaire recognized Ursula's capabilities early on and became a mentor who guided her and gave her the space to take on challenging projects. He ensured that her talents were showcased at crucial moments, positioning her for future leadership roles.

In addition to Paul Allaire, Anne Mulcahy, the CEO before Burns, became a close ally. Mulcahy, who understood the challenges of being a woman in leadership, provided Ursula with guidance and unwavering support. This mentorship turned into a powerful alliance, helping ensure Ursula's smooth transition when it was her turn to take the helm at Xerox. Having advocates like Allaire and Mulcahy within the company allowed Ursula to tackle challenges, amplify her visibility, and showcase her leadership skills.

Ursula Burns didn't stop at mentorship; she also excelled at building strategic alliances within Xerox and across the industry. These relationships played a critical role in advancing her career, especially as she prepared for her leadership transition. Burns was intentional in establishing strong connections with key stakeholders, including board members and influential industry leaders. These alliances enhanced her credibility and provided her with a healthy support network when she was appointed CEO. This network became a foundation that helped smooth her transition into leadership, ensuring she had the backing and trust of those in decision-making roles.

Burns also understood the value of looking beyond her immediate environment. She actively sought cross-industry connections by serving on the boards of major companies like American Express and Uber. By stepping into these roles, she gained insights into different industries, which in turn broadened her perspective and influence. These cross-industry connections enabled her to bring fresh ideas and approaches back to Xerox, enriching her leadership style with broader knowledge and experience. Later in her career, these experiences allowed her to transition into leadership roles beyond Xerox, applying her skills in new and diverse contexts.

Just as Ursula leveraged her connections to climb to unprecedented heights, you too can discover new paths in your career. So, challenge yourself to step out of your comfort zone. Attend a networking event, reach out to someone admired in your field, or perhaps reconnect with an old colleague whose work you respect. The key is to make this connection with purpose. Approach it with curiosity, a willingness to learn, and an openness to how this new relationship might enrich both your personal and professional growth.

Remember, visibility is about being present and engaging with others, putting yourself in spaces where your contributions are seen. So, let's take that first step, reach out, and connect.

Let's get visible.

# STRONGER TOGETHER: CREATING ALLIES AT WORK

In the early days of my career, I had the wonderful opportunity to work closely with Alicia from our pre-sales department. Her story has stayed with me ever since. She started in a role that required her to juggle multiple priorities, which included crafting proposals, meeting tight deadlines, and constantly communicating with clients. The fast pace and high expectations left little room for mistakes, and it became clear early on that this was a space where every detail mattered. But for Alicia, the challenges weren't limited to her workload. In a department dominated by men, she often found herself unsure of how to tackle the complexities of her role and her career.

It wasn't that Alicia lacked the skills or ambition—she was deeply committed to her work—but there was an undeniable sense of isolation that she couldn't shake. Without strong allies or female representation in her department, she often wondered if she was on the right path or if there was anyone who understood the unique challenges she faced.

Instead of retreating, Alicia decided to take matters into her own hands. She realized that success wasn't going to come from waiting for others to notice her efforts; she had to seek out support and build relationships that would help her grow. So, she began to forge connections beyond her immediate team. She connected with colleagues across different departments, participating in cross-functional projects and openly sharing her ideas. Little by little, these alliances opened new doors for her, providing the insights, resources, and confidence she needed to move forward.

Through these relationships, she gained valuable feedback that helped her refine her approach to handling clients. She also learned how to tackle tricky office dynamics. One of the smartest things Alicia did was seek out allies within the company. She understood that having experienced voices guiding her would make a big difference, especially in an environment where she often felt outnumbered.

At home, her success was supported by a strong network. Alicia knew she couldn't handle the pressures of work and family life without help, so she made sure she wasn't going at it alone. Her partner played a significant role, taking on household duties and caring for their child. This allowed Alicia to focus on her career without the constant worry of managing everything on her own. Whenever things got particularly hectic at work, she also relied on extended family to step in, creating a system that gave her the time and space to thrive.

Alicia's story is a clear example of how having a strong support system—both at work and at home—can help women overcome the challenges they often face in balancing career and personal life. The relationships she built with her colleagues provided her with the tools and confidence to advance in her role. Meanwhile, the support she received at home allowed her to pursue her ambitions without sacrificing her well-being. This combination of workplace allies and a supportive home life became the foundation of her success, providing the necessary boost for her hard work and helping her achieve the growth she truly deserved.

## Strength in Numbers- The Power of Allyship

What truly stood out to me from Alicia's story was the role that allies played in her success. In the professional world, especially for women, understanding allyship and embracing its potential is crucial. Allies are those who actively advocate for your growth and success, who open doors when they see potential, and who stand by you when challenges arise.

An ally can be anyone—a colleague, a leader, or even a family member. They are people who recognize the value of inclusion and take steps to promote fairness and opportunity, especially in environments where certain voices might go unheard. Whether it's a senior leader within the company or your partner at home, the presence of allies can make a significant difference in your journey.

Many people mistakenly believe that relying on others weakens independence, implying that strong women should face life's challenges solo. But that couldn't be further from the truth. As Helen Keller so wisely said, *"Alone we can do so little; together we can do so much."* True strength comes from knowing when to ask for support and understanding that success is rarely a solo effort. Allyship isn't a sign of weakness. It's a source of power, a partnership that amplifies your abilities and helps you reach your full potential.

Allies are actively involved in pushing for change. They challenge the status quo, aiming to dismantle the barriers that hold certain people back, particularly women and other marginalized groups. In organizations where power structures can sometimes be rigid, allies step in to shift the balance, creating space for underrepresented voices to be heard and valued. Their role is not passive; it involves a continuous effort to disrupt inequities and create a more inclusive environment.

But it's also important to recognize the differences between allies, mentors, and sponsors, even though their roles sometimes intersect. Mentors are those you trust for guidance, especially during critical decisions or transitions in your career. They've been there before and can offer insights based on their own experiences, helping you tackle challenges and opportunities with a clearer sense of direction.

Sponsors, on the other hand, are your champions. They're the ones speaking on your behalf when you're not in the room, advocating for your promotion, or suggesting your name for a high-visibility project. Sponsors leverage their networks and influence to open doors for you, creating opportunities that might have otherwise remained out of reach. They play a direct role in shaping your career trajectory by connecting you to new opportunities, people, and experiences.

Now, allies are a bit different. Allies often have inherent power and privilege—whether it's by being part of the majority group or holding leadership positions—and they use that privilege to advocate for those who may not have the same visibility. An ally can also be a mentor or sponsor, but their role as an ally is focused on actively challenging misconceptions, promoting fairness, and making sure those who deserve recognition receive it. Allies amplify your voice, correct biases, and ensure that you are seen and valued for your contributions.

When allies step up, they help dismantle the invisible barriers that can hold women back, barriers that often begin long before a woman is even hired. Take the recruitment process, for example. Research shows that job descriptions in male-dominated fields often use language that appeals more to men than to women. Words like "competitive," "dominant," and "leader" tend to resonate with male applicants, while more inclusive terms like "support," "understand," or "collaborative" are often overlooked. This subtle bias in language can discourage women from even applying for certain roles, limiting their chances before they've even had the opportunity to demonstrate their abilities.

Then, there's the issue of how leadership qualities are perceived. In many workplaces, assertiveness in men is seen as a positive trait—a sign of strength and confidence. But when women show the same level of assertiveness, it's often misinterpreted as being too aggressive or pushy. This double standard is one of the many ways that gender-related biases create an uneven playing field, making it harder for women to be seen as strong leaders.

And the challenges don't stop at work. At home, many women are expected to take on a larger share of household duties, from managing the home to raising children. This extra burden can make it harder to focus on building a career and accumulating the experience necessary to advance. While men are often able to dedicate more time to their jobs without the same level of responsibility at home, women are frequently left trying to juggle both, which can slow down their career progression.

Allyship can help change this. By advocating for fair hiring practices, supporting women in leadership roles, and recognizing the impact of family responsibilities, allies can make a real difference in closing the gender gap.

In addition to addressing systemic issues, allyship plays a crucial role in creating an environment where women feel like they truly belong. When women have allies in the workplace, they are less likely to feel isolated or overlooked. This sense of belonging can be transformative. It's one thing to show up to work every day, but it's another to feel confident that your voice will be heard and respected.

That kind of support changes the way you approach your work. It fuels a sense of confidence and motivates you to push beyond what you thought you were capable of. This is what allyship makes possible: a workplace where women are encouraged to thrive.

## Power in Connection

"How do allies look, and what do they do?" you might be wondering. Allies are more than just colleagues who share an office space with us. They are individuals who actively support gender equity within organizations, pushing for real change and creating spaces where women can thrive. And there is something powerful about having female allies by your side.

We've all encountered the myth that women don't support teach other at work, but that's simply not the case. Women can, and do, lift each other up, becoming some of the most reliable and influential allies you can have. Personally, I've been fortunate enough to benefit from some of the most formidable female leaders as allies in my career, especially during those early, formative years. Female allies bring something unique to the table. They understand the nuances of the challenges we face, not just as professionals but as women balancing the expectations placed on us both in and outside of work.

As Sally Helgesen and Julie Johnson wrote in The Female Vision: Women's Real Power at Work, *"Allies are different from friends in that your relationship with them always serves a specific purpose. You are trying to accomplish something, and your ally has a motive in helping you; there's a principle of mutual self-interest at work. The relationship is strategic; its purpose is to leverage power. You don't need to have a lot in common with an ally—you don't even necessarily need to enjoy one another's company—but you do need to trust one another."*

This strikes at the heart of what an ally is. It entails forging a relationship built on trust and purpose. Female allies understand your goals, support them, and have the drive to help you succeed because they know how important it is for women to rise together.

To effectively find these allies, we need to look beyond casual conversations and surface-level interactions. Building meaningful connections is key. Allies can be found throughout the organization, not just in the obvious places. Your immediate coworkers, for example, are often striving for the same goals as you. Sure, there may be moments of competition, but working together can open up mutually beneficial opportunities.

I also emphasize that peer groups can be an incredible source of support and allyship, often more valuable than we initially realize. When we surround ourselves with colleagues who share our professional goals and values, we create a network that uplifts us every day. These are the people who understand the pressures of your role because they're going through it too. They know what it feels like to face challenges, and they can offer encouragement and advice when things get tough. Having peers who are just as committed to their success as you are to yours can make all the difference, especially in a workplace that might feel isolating at times.

Building this network of supportive women can also help create a shift in how we see competition. Instead of viewing each other as rivals, we can consciously choose to collaborate and lift one another up. This mindset is especially important in work environments where the culture encourages women to compete for limited opportunities.

Looking up the ladder for allies is equally important. Senior leaders and managers have the influence and network that can really make a difference when it comes to visibility and career advancement. These are the people who interact with other high-level decision-makers and won't hesitate to highlight your strengths when the moment is right. You want allies who will not only support your growth but actively promote your contributions when you aren't in the room. That's the power of having allies in leadership positions.

Building relationships with female leaders who are dedicated to gender equity can be especially meaningful and impactful. These women often have experience tackling the same hurdles you're likely to face and can offer insights into how to handle the complexities of career advancement. They know what it's like to balance ambition with the many challenges that come with being a woman in a male-dominated space, and they've learned how to turn those challenges into opportunities.

But remember, it's important to approach these potential allies with clear intentions. We need to be intentional about what we want from these connections. It involves actively engaging in meaningful, two-way conversations where both parties benefit. A mentor or ally is most effective when there's a sense of mutual learning and growth. You may be seeking guidance, but you also have something valuable to offer—whether it's fresh ideas, new perspectives, or just an eagerness to learn. When a relationship is reciprocal, it grows significantly stronger and more meaningful.

Another key to finding strong allies is to pay attention to those who actively challenge gender biases and advocate for a more inclusive environment. Watch how potential allies react when they witness bias or discrimination—do they speak up, or stay silent? Do they make an effort to support others, or do they brush it off? The women who stand up and call out these behaviors are the ones most likely to be true allies. They're not just going along with the status quo; they're committed to making things better for all of us, and those are the people you want by your side.

It's also worth considering that sometimes we overlook potential allies because of common misconceptions. Maybe you've hesitated to seek out mentorship from another woman because you're worried it might come across as competitive, or perhaps you fear rejection. But the truth is, many women are open to offering support if we just ask. Overcoming these mental barriers is crucial. We have to be willing to reach out, show interest, and share our goals openly. You might be surprised at how many women are ready to collaborate once you take that first step.

## Recognizing Potential Allies

To make this process more tangible, let's talk about what to look for when identifying a female leader who might be an ally. These signs often go beyond the obvious and can be found in the small but telling ways a leader interacts, communicates, and engages within the organization.

One of the most subtle yet powerful signs is when a leader makes an effort to create an inclusive environment where everyone's voice is heard—especially those who might hesitate to speak up. If you're in a meeting and notice a female leader actively encouraging participation from everyone, especially women, that's a strong signal. It's even more telling when she doesn't just stop at giving the floor to someone, but truly listens and builds on their ideas. When a leader makes a point to ensure that women's contributions aren't brushed aside or overshadowed, it shows she values diverse perspectives and is committed to building an equitable workplace.

Another key indicator is when you observe a leader actively involved in initiatives focused on gender equity or diversity. Whether it's supporting a mentoring program for women or advocating for policies that make work-life balance more accessible, leaders who engage in these efforts tend to be genuinely invested in the advancement of women. Their participation in such initiatives aims to create real, lasting change. When you see a leader championing these kinds of programs, it's a clear sign that she's someone who understands the challenges women face and is willing to advocate for change.

Another important sign of a potential female ally in leadership is how willing she is to share her own story. When a leader is open about her journey—the challenges she's faced, the mistakes she's made, and how she's overcome them—it shows a level of humility and transparency that's invaluable. This kind of openness signals that she's approachable and eager to help others by sharing practical advice from her own experiences.

I've seen this in my own career—those moments when a female leader spoke candidly about the obstacles she faced as a woman in a male-dominated environment. It wasn't always the easiest conversation, but it was the kind of honesty that made me feel seen and understood. Leaders like that, who are ready to pass on what they've learned, are the ones you want as allies.

One more subtle sign of allyship lies in how a female leader recognizes and celebrates the achievements of other women. When a leader makes it a priority to publicly acknowledge the successes of women on her team, it's a powerful gesture. It boosts the visibility and credibility of women within the organization and sets a standard for valuing their contributions. I've always found that leaders who are quick to recognize the achievements of others are the ones most likely to advocate for women's career advancement.

Paying close attention to these attributes can help you identify the leaders who are likely to be the supportive allies you need on your journey.

## Broadening the Scope

It's equally important to find male allies in the workplace. One common myth about allyship is that only women can support other women, which can be misleading. While it's true that women can be incredibly powerful allies, it's equally important to acknowledge that men can play a crucial role too. Limiting allyship to women alone risks making gender equity seem like it's solely a women's issue, and that couldn't be further from the truth. If we expect meaningful, lasting change, we need everyone—regardless of gender—to be part of the solution.

The truth is, male allies are invaluable and often offer distinct advantages. Men often hold positions of influence and power in organizations, which means their voices carry weight in driving change. And while it might feel daunting at times to build these connections, I've seen firsthand how powerful male allyship can be, both in my own career and with the women I've coached.

One of the first signs of a strong male ally is their willingness to listen—really listen. Male colleagues who make an effort to understand the challenges women face in the workplace are stepping up in a meaningful way. Whether they're reading up on gender equity, attending diversity training, or simply taking the time to engage in open conversations, these men show a genuine commitment to being part of the solution. Listening is the foundation of allyship, and when a male colleague listens to your experiences without jumping to conclusions, it shows a level of respect that's crucial for real support. It also signals that he's willing to learn and grow, which is exactly what you want in an ally.

What I've found, both personally and through the stories of women I've worked with, is that men who take the time to educate themselves on these issues tend to become more invested in making things better. This proactive approach is one of the clearest indicators of a potential ally—someone who isn't just paying lip service to gender equity but is actively trying to understand how they can contribute to a more inclusive workplace.

Another key sign of a male ally is how they behave in meetings and group discussions. It's often in these settings that subtle, but powerful, acts of allyship can make all the difference. Think about how often women's voices are overshadowed or interrupted in meetings. A male ally will make a conscious effort to ensure that doesn't happen. He'll acknowledge women's contributions, give credit where it's due, and advocate for their inclusion in important conversations.

Consider this scenario: In a meeting, there is only one woman at the table. Every time she shares an idea, she is cut off or overshadowed by the male head of the committee. It's frustrating and far too common. Then, one of her male colleagues intervenes. He halts the meeting and highlights what's happening. He ensures she has the opportunity to speak without interruptions and reminds everyone to listen with an open mind. This exemplifies true allyship in action— a male colleague using his voice to amplify hers and ensuring she receives the respect she deserves.

I've seen these moments play out, and they're powerful. They send a clear message: women's voices matter, and they won't be sidelined.  But allyship doesn't stop at meetings.

Male allies often go beyond these everyday interactions and engage in public advocacy for gender equality. Whether it's speaking out against sexist behavior, supporting policies that promote work-life balance, or pushing for equal pay, men who take a stand on these issues are crucial in the fight for gender equity. Women professionals should look for male leaders who are willing to use their influence to drive meaningful change, whether by recommending qualified women for leadership roles or advocating for policies that level the playing field.

In addition to advocating for gender equity and challenging biases, male allies also build relationships with women that are rooted in mutual respect and trust. You'll often notice that true allies don't shy away from feedback—they actively seek it. They want to know how they can do better, and they're open to hearing where they might have fallen short. This openness shows a genuine desire to grow and improve as a supporter. When a male colleague asks for feedback on how he can better support you or other women, and he listens carefully without becoming defensive, that's a strong indicator that he's committed to being an effective ally.

But here's something important to keep in mind: not all allyship is created equal. It's crucial to recognize the difference between performative allyship and genuine commitment. Performative allies are those who may talk a good game but fail to follow through when it really counts. They might speak up in a meeting but disappear when it's time to advocate for you behind closed doors. True allies, on the other hand, consistently back up their words with meaningful action.

It's essential to be cautious of colleagues who say all the right things but don't demonstrate any real support or advocacy. Genuine male allies will show up for you not just when it's easy or public, but when it's difficult and when their actions can make a tangible difference. They're the ones who use their influence to make sure you have the opportunities you deserve, and they do so because they believe in fairness, not because they're looking for recognition.

By paying attention to these vital signs, you'll be able to identify who your true allies are.

## The Trust Bridge Framework

Once you've identified someone as a potential ally based on their actions and commitment, the next step is in your hands. Building trust with these allies requires consistent effort and intentionality. In the workplace, especially for women, strong alliances aren't built overnight. They're nurtured through shared goals, transparency, and regular communication. This is where my Trust Bridge Framework comes into play— designed to help women professionals create effective and productive relationships with their allies.

The first part of this framework focuses on finding ***shared goals and mutual interests***. This is essential because true alliances are built on a foundation of mutual benefit. Think about it: to establish a meaningful connection with an ally, it's important to understand their professional objectives. What are they working toward? What do they value? Once you have a sense of their priorities, you can begin to identify areas where your goals align.

Collaborating on projects that tap into both your strengths and theirs is a great way to create a sense of partnership. When both parties benefit from the relationship, the connection feels more authentic. I've seen this approach work positively for women who were struggling with visibility in their workplace. By partnering with an ally on a high-profile project, they showcased their expertise and developed a relationship of trust based on shared success. This kind of collaboration helps to break down the isolation many women face in the workplace and creates opportunities for joint achievements, which can be empowering.

The second part of the framework focuses on ***transparency and open communication***. Once you've established a shared goal with an ally, you need to maintain that connection through honesty. Transparency is what builds trust, and for women professionals, this can sometimes feel challenging. We may hesitate to fully open up about our career aspirations or the obstacles we face, but the truth is, being upfront about what you need and where you want to go is essential.

Think of it this way: when you're honest about your goals, challenges, and the type of support you're seeking, you're inviting your ally to be part of your journey. This kind of openness creates a relationship where both sides feel comfortable. That's how a real partnership grows—through clear, two-way communication. Regular check-ins can be a great way to keep that communication flowing. Whether it's a quick chat over coffee or a more formal feedback session, these moments help keep both of you aligned and ensure that the support you're offering each other is still relevant and meaningful.

I once coached a woman who had built a strong alliance with a senior colleague, but she hesitated to fully express her long-term career goals. When she finally opened up about her ambitions, not only did her ally support her, but they were able to work together more effectively, knowing exactly what they were working toward. That level of transparency transformed their partnership into something even stronger, where mutual goals became shared victories.

The third part of the framework centers on **cultivating empathy and understanding**. Empathy is the glue that deepens these connections. When you take a moment to truly listen and understand the challenges your ally faces, you create a safe space where both of you feel valued. This empathy inspires trust and makes your relationship more resilient.

Understanding your ally's perspective also helps break down some of the barriers women often face, like feeling excluded from networking opportunities or decision-making processes. It's a subtle but powerful way to challenge the systems that often leave women out of important conversations and decisions.

The next part of the framework entails **leveraging mutual support**. A truly successful alliance is built on a foundation of give and take. It's not just about what your ally can do for you; it's equally important to think about how you can support their goals. Take the time to understand what matters to them and how you might be able to contribute. It could be as simple as sharing insights from your own experience, offering feedback on a project, or connecting them with resources they might find helpful. By investing in their success, you're showing that this relationship goes both ways. This builds goodwill and often leads to your ally reciprocating in ways that benefit your career too.

And that leads us to the final part of the framework: building a network of diverse allies. It's important to remember that no single ally can provide everything you need. By cultivating a diverse network of allies across different departments, levels of seniority, and backgrounds, you tap into a rich pool of perspectives and resources. This diversity strengthens your professional network and opens doors to opportunities.

Think of your network like a web, with each connection offering something unique. One ally might help you tackle office politics, while another could offer insights into an entirely different industry or area of expertise. The broader and more diverse your network, the better equipped you are to overcome the specific challenges you face as a woman in the workplace.

When you implement the Trust Bridge Framework, you're cultivating meaningful relationships that will support your growth, boost your confidence, and help you overcome the systemic and internal challenges that often stand in the way.

## Effectively Engaging Allies

Building a relationship is one thing, but truly making the most of that alliance requires ongoing effort and strategic engagement. A great starting point is to involve your allies in formal mentorship programs. Whether you're initiating a formal program or participating in one that already exists, mentorship can be a crucial tool for professional development. It gives structure to the relationship and provides clear goals for both you and your ally. By setting regular check-ins and defining the focus of the mentorship—whether it's skill development, leadership readiness, or navigating new challenges—you ensure that the partnership stays productive and beneficial for both parties.

Another powerful way to engage your allies is through collaboration on high-impact projects. Working together on projects that are aligned with organizational goals is a fantastic way to build trust and demonstrate your value. When you take on a leadership role within these projects, you're benefiting from your ally's expertise and network. This form of collaboration boosts visibility and credibility for both you and your ally. It's a win-win situation that strengthens your bond while delivering results that matter to the organization.

Another effective way to engage your allies is by facilitating knowledge-sharing sessions. These platforms allow you to bring together your allies, along with other colleagues, to exchange insights and ideas. Organizing workshops or discussion groups where your allies share their expertise on relevant topics creates an environment of learning and collaboration. It also positions you as a leader—someone who is actively contributing to the development of others. I've seen women professionals use this strategy to break down silos within their organizations, creating opportunities for cross-departmental collaboration and creating a culture of continuous learning.

Beyond knowledge sharing, a great way to deepen your engagement with allies is through advocacy efforts. Allies can be powerful partners in driving change, especially when it comes to promoting gender equity within the workplace. By working together on diversity initiatives, participating in employee resource groups, or advocating for policy changes, you and your allies can make a real difference. And as you work together toward these broader goals, you're also reinforcing the trust and commitment that underpins your professional relationship.

## Sustaining Relationships with Allies

As our careers evolve, so do our relationships. This is especially true when it comes to our allies. Sustaining these relationships over the long term, even when career paths diverge, is crucial for us as women professionals. These alliances provide both emotional and professional support, which is essential when tackling the unique challenges we face, particularly in male-dominated industries.

One of the most important ways to maintain these connections is to develop a long-term vision for the relationship. It's easy to think of an ally as someone tied to a particular role or project, but the most meaningful relationships go beyond that. They're built on shared values and common interests that endure over time. By identifying what you and your ally both care deeply about, you create a foundation that can weather the inevitable changes in your careers.

I've seen this happen with colleagues who moved on to completely different industries or positions, yet their connection remained strong. Why? Because they focused on the bigger picture—their shared commitment to certain values like leadership development or promoting gender equity. By keeping that long-term vision in mind, their relationship remained meaningful, even as they each took on new roles.

Another way to sustain relationships with allies when career paths diverge is by finding opportunities for cross-industry collaboration. Just because you and your ally aren't working in the same space anymore doesn't mean you can't still benefit from each other's expertise. In fact, sometimes stepping outside your usual environment can spark innovative ideas. You might consider co-authoring articles, developing workshops, or brainstorming on interdisciplinary projects that leverage your different experiences and skills.

These kinds of collaborations keep the relationship active and give both of you fresh perspectives that can enhance your professional growth. They also open the door to new possibilities, expanding your networks and introducing you to ideas that you might not have encountered within the confines of your own industry.

Another way to ensure long-term growth with your allies is to formalize the relationship by creating a mentorship exchange. It's about recognizing that, as women professionals, we have a lot to learn from each other, regardless of our respective industries or seniority levels. When you set up this reciprocal arrangement, you create a space for continuous learning and mutual support. You're both able to adapt to one another's evolving needs while expanding your perspectives.

Beyond mentorship, one way to stay connected and keep the relationship dynamic is to engage in strategic networking together. Even if your fields have drifted apart, attending industry events or conferences together can be incredibly powerful. These shared experiences allow you to tap into new ideas and opportunities, while also strengthening your bond. I've always believed that showing up for each other in these spaces deepens your relationship and opens up fresh collaborations that you might not have expected.

For instance, I once worked with two professionals who used to be in the same company but went on to work in very different industries. They made it a point to attend at least one major conference together each year. Over time, they began introducing each other to key contacts from their respective fields, creating a bridge between their industries that led to cross-sector projects and opportunities for both of them. That's the power of strategic networking—it multiplies your opportunities by extending your reach across multiple networks.

And when geography or time makes it difficult to meet in person, technology is your best ally. Virtual collaboration tools can be a game-changer in maintaining a productive relationship, even when distance or professional differences come into play. Whether it's through project management software or just regular virtual meetings, these tools allow you to stay engaged, working on joint initiatives that keep the relationship moving forward.

Beyond personal growth, a powerful way to strengthen an alliance is by advocating for systemic change together. Many of the challenges women face in the workplace are rooted in broader systemic issues, and working with an ally to address these problems can create a lasting impact. Whether it's through diversity initiatives, community outreach programs, or pushing for policy changes, aligning on broader goals allows you both to take the relationship to another level. This kind of collaboration brings real value to the relationship because it taps into shared passions while also having a tangible impact. Working toward a common cause solidifies the partnership, ensuring that it continues to thrive and remains significant beyond the day-to-day work.

These enduring alliances have the potential to create broader changes in the workplace and even within entire industries. When we come together with intention and mutual support, we begin to shift the dynamics, challenging outdated norms and opening doors for the next generation of women professionals.

As writer Isabel Allende so beautifully said, *"I can promise you that women working together—linked, informed, and educated—can bring peace and prosperity to this forsaken planet."* Her words uphold the collective power we have when we nurture our relationships and work toward shared goals.

So, I encourage you to take the first step today. Begin with small, genuine actions that pave the way for meaningful connections. Maybe it's reaching out to a colleague whose work you respect and offering a few words of encouragement. Perhaps you invite someone for a coffee chat and learn about their experiences. These simple acts of appreciation and curiosity can lead to deeper conversations and valuable partnerships.

Engage with purpose, knowing that through these relationships, we can achieve far more together than we ever could alone. The power of allyship is real, and it's yours to embrace. Together, we can lift each other up, create lasting change, and build a legacy that empowers every woman to step into her greatness.

# CHAPTER 10

# LIFT AS YOU CLIMB: INSPIRING A CULTURE OF SUPPORT AMONG WOMEN

Lailah Gifty Akita once shared something that really speaks to me: "We are what our great mentors have taught us." When I reflect on my own journey, these words hold even more weight. As a woman climbing the corporate ladder, I didn't have many women role models to look up to. It was a male-dominated space, and there were few examples of female leadership to guide me. But that absence made me even more determined to be the mentor I wished I had for other women following the same path. I've made it a priority in my life to mentor and advocate for other women, encouraging them to reach their potential and embrace leadership roles. I see this as a way of giving back and as a crucial strategy for closing the gender gap in business.

In a male-dominated workplace, mentorship offers women something invaluable: guidance on how to tackle challenges unique to their experience. Gender bias and stereotypes are obstacles many women face, and mentors who have been through similar situations can offer advice that comes from lived experience. They've walked that path, faced those biases, and found ways to challenge stereotypes without alienating colleagues or jeopardizing relationships. That's what makes mentorship so powerful—when you see someone who looks like you, who's faced similar challenges and succeeded, it becomes easier to imagine yourself in those leadership roles. This kind of representation is incredibly important, especially in fields where female role models are few and far between.

Beyond inspiration, mentorship is also about guidance—real, actionable guidance that can help clarify career pathways. Many women find themselves at crossroads in their careers, unsure of which direction to take or what opportunities are worth pursuing. A mentor can help define and refine your goals, offering perspectives you may not have considered before. They've been where you are, and they can help you tackle the decision-making process, whether it's choosing to further your education, negotiating job offers, or deciding when it's time to pursue a promotion.

This personalized guidance is often the key to unlocking new opportunities. Mentors understand the complexities of balancing ambition with the realities of workplace dynamics. They can help you make strategic decisions that align with your strengths and aspirations, offering you a clearer sense of where you're headed and how to get there. In many organizations, mentorship has become a central part of diversity, equity, and inclusion (DEI) efforts. It's no secret that women—particularly those from marginalized groups—are underrepresented in leadership roles. Just 53 female CEOs lead Fortune 500 companies, and the number is even smaller when you consider women from diverse backgrounds. Mentorship programs can help change this. Women with mentors have more opportunities for advancement, and when they do, they're more likely to stay with their organizations. It's a win for both the individual and the company.

Mentorship is also about building resilience. In environments where women are underrepresented, having a mentor can provide the support you need to stay grounded and confident. When you know someone is in your corner, it gives you a sense of psychological safety, something that's essential in workplaces where you may otherwise feel isolated. This emotional connection, especially when women mentor other women, has become so impactful that the term "femtors" has gained popularity. It captures the unique perspective and bond that often forms when women mentor each other, providing both career guidance and solidarity.

These relationships inspire mutual growth and, ultimately, contribute to a workplace culture that values and uplifts everyone. I've seen this firsthand with my friend Kamala.

Kamala, a friend from my college days, found herself working in the dev department of a fast-paced, male-dominated tech company. Like many women in similar environments, Kamala faced challenges that felt overwhelming at times. She often felt isolated, unsure of how to assert her ideas in meetings where louder voices dominated the conversation. Worse, her contributions were frequently overshadowed by those of her male colleagues, leaving her frustrated and questioning her path forward.

But Kamala wasn't one to give up easily. Recognizing that something needed to change, she decided to seek out guidance. That's when she found her mentor—a senior female executive in the company who had already tackled many of the hurdles Kamala was facing. This connection turned out to be the turning point in her career. Through regular mentoring sessions, Kamala's mentor helped her gain clarity on how to manage the dynamics of the workplace. They talked about everything from how to communicate her ideas more effectively to strategies for overcoming the biases that often lingered beneath the surface.

What made this mentorship so impactful was the personalized advice and the sense of support. Kamala's mentor became a trusted source of encouragement, helping Kamala build confidence where it had once been lacking. Together, they discussed strategies for self-advocacy, and slowly, Kamala began to see a shift in how she presented herself at work.

One of the most transformative aspects of their relationship was when Kamala's mentor began introducing her to key people within the company. Suddenly, Kamala's network expanded in ways she had never anticipated. Her mentor leveraged her own connections to ensure Kamala was seen, not just heard, and doors started to open. This sponsorship was crucial to ensure Kamala's talents were recognized and nurtured.

Kamala's mentor also turned out to be a vital source of emotional support, playing a key role in helping her build confidence. Knowing that someone genuinely understood her challenges and believed in her potential made all the difference. With her mentor's encouragement, Kamala began to take on more challenging projects, ones that highlighted her technical skills and leadership abilities. These opportunities allowed her to stand out and gain the recognition she deserved from management.

As Kamala's confidence grew, so did her willingness to advocate for herself. With her mentor's guidance, she negotiated a promotion to a team lead position—a vital moment in her career. In this new role, Kamala put into practice many of the inclusive strategies she had learned from her mentor. She nurtured a collaborative environment, ensuring that all voices on her team were heard, just as she had once longed for herself.

## Finding the Right Mentor: A Path to Growth

Kamala's story shows us just how transformative mentorship can be. Having the right mentor can make all the difference in your career. But you might be wondering, how do you even begin finding such a person? The journey of seeking out a mentor may feel unfamiliar or even daunting, but it's a crucial step toward building the support network you need to thrive in your professional life.

At its core, mentorship is about building a relationship with someone who actively invests in your development, someone who listens, challenges you to grow, and helps you see new possibilities. And here's the important part: a mentor doesn't have to be someone older, or in a high-ranking position. What truly matters is finding someone whose values align with yours and whose experiences inspire you.

So how do you identify the right mentor? A great starting point is to identify someone whose work ethic, values, and skills you admire. Think about colleagues, leaders, or even individuals outside of your immediate network who exemplify the qualities you hope to develop. The connection can be as simple as noticing how they handle difficult situations or the confidence they exhibit at the workplace.

Equally vital is ensuring that the way they communicate and interact aligns with your own preferences. Too often, we overlook these aspects. I've seen situations where mentorship relationships start strong but falter because of a misalignment in communication. Imagine a potential mentor who is direct and assertive in their feedback, but you, as a mentee, thrive in environments that encourage a more collaborative and gentle approach. This difference may create friction over time, making it hard to build a productive and fulfilling mentorship. It's essential, therefore, to observe how potential mentors communicate and ask yourself if this is a style that will help you grow. Finding someone whose approach makes you feel comfortable yet challenged is key.

Another important aspect is to seek out mentors who have successfully overcome challenges that mirror your own. For many women, these challenges might include balancing career growth with personal life, dealing with gender bias in the workplace, or navigating a career path in industries traditionally dominated by men. A mentor who has faced and overcome these same hurdles will be uniquely equipped to offer advice that goes beyond the generic.

Let's also talk about influence—something that many women tend to overlook. It's easy to focus on a mentor's personal accomplishments without considering the doors they might be able to open for you. A well-connected mentor can offer much more than advice. They can introduce you to key individuals within your organization or industry, advocate for your growth, and position you for opportunities that might not be visible to you yet.

Finding a mentor is also about connecting with someone who truly understands the challenges that women professionals face. That's why looking for a mentor who is committed to diversity and inclusion can make all the difference. A mentor who actively champions these values will likely be more in tune with the specific barriers women encounter in the workplace. They'll have a clearer perspective on issues like gender bias, work-life balance, and the complexities of advancing in male-dominated environments.

Another key strategy is to gather feedback from peers or colleagues about potential mentors. Don't be afraid to ask others for their experiences with a particular mentor. Hearing first-hand stories about their mentoring style, reliability, and overall approach can provide valuable insights that aren't always visible from the outside. Doing a bit of this due diligence" can help you ensure that you're selecting someone who is not only aligned with your goals but also has a track record of being an effective mentor.

And perhaps most importantly, trust your instincts. While it's essential to do the research, observe potential mentors, and gather feedback, sometimes you'll just have a gut feeling about someone. If something feels off, or if you're hesitating, that could be a sign that this particular mentor isn't the best fit for you. Conversely, when you feel drawn toward someone's approach or leadership style, it's worth exploring that connection further. Your intuition is often a powerful guide in determining whether a mentorship relationship will be fruitful.

When all of these pieces are aligned, you'll find a mentor who supports your growth and truly empowers you to tackle the challenges that come your way.

## The Empowerment Framework: Building a Meaningful Mentor-Mentee Relationship

Developing a deep, meaningful connection with a mentor involves creating a relationship that nurtures growth and builds confidence. In my journey of forging meaningful relationships with mentors, I was introduced to the early version of what I now call the Empowerment Framework by one of my mentors. At the time, it wasn't formalized, but the essence of it was there. Over the years, I found myself building upon these principles, refining and shaping them based on experiences. What I'm sharing with you today is a version of that framework that's evolved from those early lessons, and I hope it serves you as well as it's served me.

At the heart of the Empowerment Framework is trust. Without trust, any relationship, especially one as important as mentorship, will struggle to flourish. Trust starts with transparency and open communication, which creates a space where both the mentor and mentee feel comfortable sharing successes, challenges, uncertainties, and fears. This kind of openness lays the foundation for mutual respect. As a mentee, when you communicate your aspirations, struggles, and ambitions with vulnerability, you open the door to more tailored, valuable guidance from your mentor.

One key component of this framework is active listening. Your mentor's wisdom is rooted in years of experience, so listening attentively, asking follow-up questions, and reflecting on the advice shared allows you to benefit from their journey in a way that is directly relevant to your own path.

Establishing clear, collaborative objectives is another essential part of this framework. Sit down with your mentor and outline the specific goals you want to achieve, both short-term and long-term. This may include developing certain skills, handling office dynamics, or advancing toward a leadership role. By defining these objectives together, you ensure that your meetings and interactions stay focused and purposeful. Regular check-ins are crucial to revisit these goals, assess progress, and recalibrate as needed. This continuous dialogue keeps both parties aligned and ensures that the relationship remains dynamic and productive.

The next part of the Empowerment Framework is embracing vulnerability. It's natural to feel hesitant about sharing your struggles, especially in a professional setting where competence is often emphasized. However, being open about your challenges allows your mentor to give you more targeted, practical advice. When you share the full scope of your situation—whether it's feeling isolated in meetings, struggling with work-life balance, or dealing with imposter syndrome—your mentor can provide insights that are directly applicable to the obstacles you're facing.

In building a meaningful mentor-mentee relationship, one of the most transformative steps is seeking feedback. For many of us, feedback can feel intimidating, especially in environments where we've been conditioned to see criticism as something personal. But when we approach it with an open mind, it becomes an invaluable tool for growth. Encouraging honest feedback from a mentor shows that we're committed to learning and evolving. A mentor who feels safe giving us constructive advice will often become more invested in our progress, knowing we're willing to grow and make real changes.

Taking initiative is just as important. We need to be the ones who keep the relationship active. It's easy to fall into the habit of waiting for our mentor to reach out, but real success comes from being proactive. Setting up regular meetings, coming prepared with thoughtful questions, and being open to their suggestions all show that we value the time and effort our mentor is putting in. When we take responsibility for moving the process forward, we keep the momentum going and ensure that both sides are engaged in a meaningful way.

One of the most overlooked aspects of mentorship is the power of the mentor's network. Sometimes, we get so focused on the one-on-one guidance that we forget about the opportunities that can come from connecting with others in their circle. These introductions can lead to new collaborations, career opportunities, or even just different perspectives that we hadn't considered before. It's important to express interest in meeting these contacts and explore how they might open new doors for us.

And finally, we can't forget to show appreciation. Mentors give us their time, share their wisdom, and often provide access to their networks, all of which are invaluable. Taking a moment to recognize this investment through a simple thank you or acknowledgment can deepen the relationship in ways that are both personal and lasting. Gratitude goes a long way in keeping that connection strong.

## How Sponsorship Opens Doors

In addition to mentorship, there's another equally important facet to career growth that often doesn't get as much attention: sponsorship. While we frequently hear about the importance of mentorship, we need to have an equally strong conversation around sponsorship. Mentorship, sponsorship, and allyship intersect in many ways, but sponsorship plays a unique and powerful role in opening doors for career advancement. When I think back on my own career, I realize how instrumental sponsorship was in helping me reach higher levels. Mentors provided guidance, but it was sponsors who truly opened doors—introducing me to decision-makers, pushing my name forward when opportunities arose, and making sure my work was seen..

Sponsorship is different from mentorship because it goes beyond offering advice. It's about someone with influence advocating for your success and creating opportunities that may not otherwise be accessible. A sponsor actively works to ensure your visibility in front of key players within the organization. They speak up for you in meetings, recommend you for critical projects, and promote you when leadership discussions happen.

Think about it: How many times have you worked hard on something but felt it went unnoticed? How often did you wonder what it would take for someone to really see your potential? This is where sponsorship comes in. A sponsor ensures that your hard work isn't invisible. They create opportunities for you to be seen by those who matter, which is often the key to unlocking new levels of responsibility, pay, and influence.

The challenges women face, highlighted by the World Economic Forum's Global Gender Gap Report, make sponsorship more critical than ever. Despite more women entering paid work and leadership roles, societal expectations and workplace policies continue to hold many women back—especially those with caregiving responsibilities. In this harsh economic situation, exacerbated by geopolitical conflicts and larger changes that disproportionately affect women, having a sponsor can be truly transformative.

As I reflect on the power of sponsorship, one striking observation from Sylvia Ann Hewlett, a global expert in talent innovation, stands out: women are 54% less likely than men to have a sponsor. This gap speaks volumes about the hurdles women face in reaching higher levels within their careers. Sponsorship, as Hewlett suggests, can be the key to unlocking doors that might otherwise remain closed.

All of these opportunities fast-track our careers, equipping us with essential skills and connections. Studies show that women with sponsors are 20% more likely to be promoted than those without.

This is why having a sponsor is about so much more than personal career advancement. It's about changing the world for all of us—pushing for a future where success is based on merit, and where women can rise to the top without having to break through barriers every step of the way.

## Finding the Right Sponsor

Finding the right sponsor is where the journey truly begins. When I first sought out a sponsor, it wasn't immediately clear where to look or how to start. But through trial and error and a bit of guidance, I found supportive sponsors who played a key role in shaping my growth and career journey, helping me become the professional I am today. Here is a glimpse into what helped me.

To begin, finding the right sponsor means looking beyond the surface. You're searching for someone who has influence—someone whose voice carries weight in your organization or industry. But there's more to it. A sponsor should also have a proven history of advocating for others. You want someone who has already shown they're committed to helping others succeed, especially women and underrepresented groups. Think about the leaders you've seen who actively promote initiatives around diversity and inclusion. These are the people who are likely to understand your unique challenges and have the power to help you navigate them.

It's not always about finding the most senior person in the room. It's about identifying someone with the authority to advocate for you in meaningful ways, whether it's recommending you for a high-profile project or ensuring your contributions are recognized in important discussions. Look for leaders who have been vocal about gender equality, those who sponsor initiatives that lift others up. That's a sign that they'll be willing to champion your growth as well.

The key here is to observe. Watch how potential sponsors interact with others. Are they the kind of leader who steps in to support when someone's voice isn't being heard? Do they make room for others at the table? This will give you a sense of whether they have the qualities needed in a sponsor who can advocate for your advancement in a real and impactful way.

Another vital thing I learned was the importance of finding a sponsor who could open doors. It wasn't enough for them to simply be in a position of power—they needed to have the ability to connect me to the right people and projects.

You want a sponsor who can introduce you to key players within your organization and beyond. These introductions can be transformative, offering you access to high-impact opportunities that can change the course of your career.

Equally important is finding someone with credibility. A sponsor who is respected within the organization will have a far greater impact when they advocate for you. Their endorsement carries weight because they've built a reputation for integrity and leadership. That's why it's essential to observe how your potential sponsor is perceived by others. Are they admired by their peers? Do they hold influence when decisions are being made? These are the qualities that make a sponsor's advocacy powerful.

Choosing the right sponsor who truly embodies these qualities can really boost your career. It helps make sure that your contributions and potential get the recognition and support they deserve.

## The Sponsorship Synergy

Engaging sponsors effectively is crucial for advancing your career, especially when you're tackling the complexities of the professional world as a woman. This process entails creating and nurturing relationships that matter. I've learned that there are two critical elements to this engagement: performance currency and relationship currency.

Performance currency, as described by Carla Harris, a senior client advisor at Morgan Stanley, is earned by delivering exceptional work and exceeding expectations. Early in your career, this is what helps you stand out—it's what gets you noticed. Consistently going above and beyond shows sponsors that you're capable and ready to take on more responsibilities. For many of us, this is where we naturally shine. We know how to perform, and we've likely been doing it all our lives, striving to meet high standards.

However, as you progress, performance alone may not be enough. Over time, the value of performance currency starts to level off because delivering great work becomes expected—it's your new normal. While it's still important to maintain this high standard, it's no longer the primary way to move ahead. This is where relationship currency comes into play.

Relationship currency is about building trust and meaningful connections with the right people. These are the relationships that will open doors to opportunities you might not even know exist. It involves making sure that the people who can help you advance know who you are and trust your abilities. Sometimes, we can get so focused on performing well that we forget the importance of these relationships. But in many cases, decisions about promotions, projects, or other significant opportunities are influenced by the strength of these personal connections.

Building relationship currency starts with intentionality. Get to know the people in positions of influence within your organization. Understand their values, what they care about, and how your contributions can align with their goals. Engage in regular, meaningful interactions—whether that's in meetings, casual conversations, or collaborative projects. Demonstrate how your work supports the broader objectives of the organization.

Carla Harris herself is a prime example of how these principles work in practice. During her time on Wall Street,

Harris showed that while delivering strong results is essential, building relationships is what moves your career forward. She encourages women to focus on excelling in their roles while also investing in meaningful connections with potential sponsors. By understanding what these sponsors care about and aligning her contributions with their goals, Harris built trust and gained advocates for her career. Through her balance of delivering high performance and nurturing relationships, she was able to secure sponsors who supported her advancement, helping her land key leadership roles and take on high-visibility projects.

## Lifting as You Climb

Michelle Obama once said, "One person might be senior and be wiser and have more experience, but I've learned a lot from the people I mentor." Her words really reflect my own experiences of working with amazing women. Mentoring others, particularly women who are navigating their own career paths, has been just as enriching for me as it has for them. When we take on the role of a mentor as women leaders, we open ourselves up to growth, new perspectives, and a more profound understanding of the work we do.

When we, as women in leadership, actively mentor and sponsor others, we contribute to a larger movement toward inclusivity in our workplaces. Our role isn't just about guiding one individual. We help create a culture where diverse voices are heard, valued, and uplifted. And when women mentor and sponsor other women, they champion gender equality, often advocating for broader systemic changes that help level the playing field for all underrepresented groups. This kind of advocacy makes organizations more innovative and collaborative, which benefits everyone.

Take the example of organizations like Lean In Circles, founded by Sheryl Sandberg. These groups offer women a space for mentorship, support, and encouragement. By nurturing connections and facilitating guidance, Lean In Circles have helped thousands of women gain the skills and confidence they need to break barriers in their careers. This shows that structured mentorship and sponsorship can be transformative tools, empowering women to rise and thrive in spaces that may have once felt unreachable.

Mentorship and sponsorship then become a ripple effect, creating lasting change across industries and organizations and shaping a future where women can reach new heights with the support of those who've gone before them.

## Stepping Up as a Mentor

Stepping into the role of a mentor can feel a bit overwhelming at first. You might wonder if you're truly ready to guide someone else or if you have enough wisdom to share. But I can tell you, from my own experience, that it's a journey well worth taking. Mentoring is incredibly rewarding. Over the years, I've learned so much from the women I've mentored, and those experiences have made me a better leader.

From my own mentorship journey, I've come across some key aspects that have proven helpful, both for me and for the women I've worked with. These insights can be a good starting point as you begin mentoring others and create a real impact. One of the most important things I've learned is that creating a safe and trusting environment is essential. It's about being approachable and showing empathy, making sure your mentees feel comfortable enough to share their challenges and goals without fear of judgment.

When you build that trust, the mentorship becomes more meaningful. Your mentees will open up about the real struggles they're facing, and that's where you can offer the most support. Building confidence is another key part of effective mentorship, and it often starts with pushing mentees beyond their comfort zones. As women leaders, we can guide our mentees by encouraging them to take on projects that challenge their skills. These are the moments when real growth happens. When a mentee takes on a leadership role or a challenging assignment, it allows her to see her own potential more clearly. And while it's important to push them towards growth, it's equally important to celebrate their wins along the way. Recognizing their successes, no matter how small, reinforces their confidence and belief in their own abilities.

Another aspect that has a huge impact on career development is the power of networking. One of the most valuable things you can offer as a mentor is introducing your mentee to key people in your network. These connections can be the bridge to new opportunities—whether it's a promotion, a career shift, or even a collaboration that helps them gain visibility. I've seen firsthand how introducing someone to the right contact can transform their career trajectory, and it's something we, as mentors, can do with ease.

But mentorship also goes beyond the individual. As women in leadership, we have the responsibility to push for systemic changes that make the workplace more inclusive for all women. This might mean advocating for a formal mentoring program that targets high-potential women within your organization. I've seen companies like Keysight, for example, create dedicated programs such as Women in Quantum, which support women in leadership and have also earned recognition for their effectiveness.

## How Women Leaders Can Sponsor Future Leaders

Stepping into the role of a sponsor as a woman leader can feel like a big responsibility as it entails actively helping to create opportunities for other women to grow, advance, and thrive in their careers.

To start being an effective sponsor, it's essential to look out for women who have potential but haven't yet been fully seen. Often, great talent can be overlooked because it doesn't fit the traditional mold. As sponsors, our role is to find those women who may not yet have had the platform to showcase their skills and to help bring their work and potential into the spotlight. It's about creating a more diverse leadership pipeline by giving talented women a chance to shine.

Once you've identified someone you believe in, the next step is to connect with her on a deeper level by really understanding her career goals, her strengths, and the challenges she's tackling. Having open and honest conversations will help ensure that the opportunities you advocate for match her ambitions and needs. Sponsorship is most powerful when it's personal, when you're genuinely invested in her growth and working to align your influence with her aspirations.

Furthermore, a big part of our role involves introducing these rising stars to key players within and outside our organizations. Expanding their network opens doors to new opportunities that might have been out of reach. This strategic visibility can make all the difference in building their career trajectory and leadership presence.

Another key role we play is in advocating for our protégés during performance reviews and promotion discussions. It's here that we must highlight their achievements and potential, making sure decision-makers are aware of their contributions and capabilities. By doing so, we help dismantle the common barriers that often hold women back, such as unconscious bias or simple invisibility in key discussions.

In addition to breaking barriers for others, it's crucial that we model the behavior we advocate by embodying inclusive leadership. Our actions can set a standard, showing others the value of diversity and sponsorship. Being open about our sponsorship efforts and sharing the successes of those we've helped advance can catalyze a culture shift within the organization, promoting a more supportive and inclusive environment.

Lastly, sponsorship is a relationship that continues over time. It's about staying connected and offering guidance as your protégé progresses. Regular check-ins give you the chance to offer advice as new challenges arise and to help them adjust their strategies as they grow. This ongoing support is what makes sponsorship so impactful—not just a one-time push, but a continuous commitment to someone's development.

I've seen how this ripple grows. When a woman benefits from mentorship or sponsorship, she is more likely to pass that support on, helping others in turn. This creates a cycle of empowerment where women are not just climbing the ladder for themselves but are actively reaching back to help others climb as well.

So, whether you're seeking out a mentor or sponsor to help guide you, or you're ready to step into those roles yourself, now is the time to take action. Reach out to someone whose work inspires you. Or, if you're in a leadership position, identify and nurture the potential in the women around you. Your first step can make all the difference. Let's start today.

# CHAPTER 11

# HARMONY AT WORK AND HOME: MASTERING THE BALANCING ACT

Let me tell you about someone I've always found inspiring. Alia, a close friend of mine, started her career as a Business Analyst with all the drive and enthusiasm you could imagine. Like many of us, she had big goals and was determined to make her mark professionally. But she didn't want her success to come at the expense of her personal life. She dreamed of finding that elusive balance between a career she loved and a personal life that felt just as fulfilling.

At first, things didn't go as planned. Alia found herself pouring every ounce of energy into her job, and slowly but surely, her work-life balance tipped too far in one direction. Long hours, high-pressure projects, and endless deadlines began to take over her days. Weekends bled into workdays, and time for herself or her family slipped away. It wasn't long before the strain started showing, both in her health and her happiness. Alia realized that despite her professional accomplishments, something was missing. She wasn't just tired—she was burning out.

It was a tough wake-up call, but it gave her the clarity she needed. Alia took a step back and reevaluated where things were headed. She sought advice from a mentor who had walked a similar path and found ways to balance career success with personal well-being. Her mentor's guidance was a turning point, helping Alia realize the importance of setting boundaries and making self-care a priority.

With this newfound insight, she began making small changes that slowly transformed her life. Alia started setting clear work hours and made it a point to leave the office at a reasonable time each day. She integrated simple routines such as regular exercise and mindfulness into her daily life, finding that these changes eased her stress and gave her more control over her time.

Alia's journey wasn't without its share of challenges. As she began to carve out time for herself and set clearer boundaries between work and personal life, not everyone was on board. Some of her male colleagues, unfortunately, expressed skepticism. Remarks like "Are you sure you can handle this project?" or "Isn't this too much for you?" popped up more than once. It was a subtle but persistent questioning of her commitment. It wasn't that they doubted her capability; it was the ingrained notion that seeking balance somehow equaled a lack of dedication.

But Alia wasn't deterred. She stood firm in her resolve, recognizing that balance was essential for her well-being and success. What helped her push through this skepticism were the allies she found along the way—both men and women— who understood the value of balance. They supported her decisions and encouraged her to maintain the boundaries she set, reinforcing that pursuing a balanced life didn't make her any less of a professional.

As time passed, the benefits of Alia's commitment to balance became apparent. She was more focused and productive at work, largely because she was no longer constantly drained or stretched too thin. Her personal life, too, began to flourish. She had time for her family, friends, and even for herself—something that had been missing before. With this renewed sense of balance, Alia experienced a deeper fulfillment, one that permeated every aspect of her life.

Alia's story serves as a powerful reminder of what's possible when women advocate for their needs and challenge the biases that suggest balance isn't achievable.

## The Pursuit of Balance

While Alia's story is indeed inspiring, it's important to recognize that her journey toward achieving balance wasn't a straight line. The struggles she faced—feeling overwhelmed by her career, fighting against burnout, and learning to set boundaries—are experiences that resonate with many women across industries. In fact, this constant juggling act is a familiar narrative for women professionals all over the world, from corporate boardrooms to startups.

Work-life balance is often portrayed as an ideal state, something we all strive for, where our careers and personal lives seamlessly coexist. But for many women, balance feels more like an illusion, a distant goal that's harder to grasp due to the unique challenges they face. Between professional duties and personal responsibilities, it can seem like there's always something pulling you in multiple directions at once. And for women, this pressure is often magnified by the fact that many industries were historically built with male professionals in mind. The norms, expectations, and unwritten rules still reflect that bias.

Despite the progress women have made in breaking glass ceilings and pushing boundaries in the workforce, the quest for balance remains difficult. Societal expectations still lean heavily on women to carry the load of domestic responsibilities, and this imbalance can create even more pressure. In many homes, women are expected to be both the primary caregivers and high-achieving professionals, and trying to manage both can feel overwhelming.

The COVID-19 pandemic underscored these disparities. As remote work became the norm, the line between professional and personal life practically disappeared, making it even harder for women to find breathing room. A report from the UN revealed that during the pandemic, women bore the majority of household chores and caregiving duties, often while still managing full-time careers.

This growing imbalance is further intensified by workplace cultures that may not fully support flexible working arrangements or acknowledge the unique needs of women. For example, a recent survey conducted by Bloom UK in February 2024 revealed that more than 93% of women have experienced mental health issues as a direct result of poor work-life balance. This survey, which included 704 women in the marketing and communications industry, paints a clear picture of the toll these imbalances take on personal lives.

More than two-fifths of the respondents reported experiencing stress, anxiety, or burnout, all stemming from an inability to manage their workload effectively. Additionally, over half of the women surveyed admitted that they frequently felt overwhelmed by their professional responsibilities. These challenges are only intensified for women from diverse backgrounds. For instance, many South Asian women report feeling especially burdened by work demands, a reflection of the cultural expectations and family responsibilities that often intersect with career pressures. This added layer of complexity makes achieving balance even more elusive for some.

Gender bias and workplace discrimination further complicate this pursuit of balance. Many women find themselves working harder to prove their competence, battling against persistent stereotypes about their capabilities. These biases limit career progression and create a cycle of overworking to meet expectations, often at the expense of personal well-being. The constant need to perform at elevated levels leads to a heavier burden, particularly for those striving to excel in male-dominated industries.

This pressure takes a personal toll as well. For many women, the challenge of balancing high expectations at work with personal commitments becomes overwhelming. This is where the need for a healthy work-life balance comes into sharp focus. Without balance, the pressures of work and personal life can lead to chronic stress, sleep problems, and even long-term health risks like cardiovascular diseases. These issues often affect women more because of the multiple roles they take on, both professionally and personally. Without the right support and enough time to rest and recharge, the consequences can be serious.

When women achieve a harmonious balance between their professional and personal lives, the benefits are manifold. It equips them to manage stress more adeptly, boosts their overall health, and directly translates to heightened job performance.

## Time as a Tool

The journey toward achieving work-life balance often begins with something so simple yet so essential—effective time management. It's one of the first pillars for women professionals who are trying to balance both their personal and professional lives. Mastering how we manage our time can set the tone for everything that follows, helping us feel in control and create space for what truly matters in both work and home life.

One of the challenges women face in this journey is the external and internal biases that shape how time is managed. In many cases, workplace biases can make it difficult for women to manage their time efficiently. For example, women are sometimes overlooked for leadership roles or high-profile projects because of assumptions about their availability or commitment—particularly if they have caregiving responsibilities. This bias forces many women into roles that are less critical to their professional growth. When you're spending more time proving yourself in these roles, the imbalance grows, and it becomes even harder to focus on the opportunities that truly align with your career goals.

Beyond the workplace, many of us wrestle with our own internal biases—the societal expectations that tell us we need to excel in every sphere. This pressure can lead to a constant balancing act, where perfectionism takes over. We hesitate to ask for help, thinking we should be able to handle it all, or we avoid setting boundaries for fear of being seen as less committed. As a result, many women overcommit and feel stretched thin, which impacts how efficiently time is spent both at work and at home.

Additionally, many of us tend to make missteps when it comes to managing time effectively. One common challenge is the struggle to prioritize tasks. It's easy to get caught in the mindset that everything is urgent, which leads to spreading ourselves too thin and tackling every task with the same level of urgency. This approach drains our energy and often leaves us feeling burnt out and unproductive by the end of the day.

Another frequent issue is the inclination to say "yes" to everything. Whether it's taking on additional work projects, helping colleagues, or managing social and family obligations, many of us fall into the habit of agreeing to more than we can reasonably handle. Over time, this habit leaves little space for personal interests or self-care, which are crucial for maintaining both physical and mental well-being.

By becoming more strategic in how we allocate our time, we can start to break away from external expectations and the internal pressures we place on ourselves. This allows us to manage both our personal commitments and professional responsibilities in a way that brings a sense of balance.

In taking control of time, we also reclaim control of our lives—creating space for meaningful work, personal fulfillment, and everything in between. It's not easy, but with the right mindset and tools, it's certainly possible.

## The Eisenhower Matrix

Time management, as Marie Curie once noted, has always been a delicate balancing act. She famously said, "I have frequently been questioned, especially by women, of how I could reconcile family life with a scientific career. Well, it has not been easy." This statement resonates deeply because it acknowledges the challenge women face when trying to balance the many facets of life—professional, personal, and everything in between. Managing time effectively is far from easy, but it's also something that can be approached strategically.

For women professionals who are striving for better work-life balance, one powerful tool to consider is the Eisenhower Matrix. The Eisenhower Matrix is deceptively simple, but its impact can be profound when applied correctly. It categorizes tasks into four key areas: Urgent & Important, Important but Not Urgent, Urgent but Not Important, and Not Urgent & Not Important. For those of us trying to juggle everything, this framework helps to clear the noise, focusing attention on what truly matters and letting go of what doesn't.

By using this matrix, you can begin to view your tasks through a more intentional lens, asking yourself questions like: What absolutely needs my attention today? What can be scheduled for later? And perhaps most liberating, what can be delegated or even eliminated? It's about learning to focus your energy where it can have the most significant impact, while freeing yourself from unnecessary burdens.

Let's dive a little deeper into the different elements of the Eisenhower Matrix, and how each one can make a tangible difference in your day-to-day life.

The first quadrant—Urgent & Important tasks—requires immediate attention. These are the tasks that are essential to reaching your goals and can't be pushed off. As women, we often find ourselves juggling these with personal responsibilities, which can lead to feeling stretched too thin. There's a tendency to fear being seen as less committed at work if personal priorities occasionally take precedence. But the beauty of this matrix is that it encourages us to handle these tasks promptly while ensuring we have the right support systems in place, whether at home or in the office, to make it all manageable.

The second quadrant—Important but Not Urgent—is often overlooked, and yet it holds the key to long-term growth. These are the tasks that will help you develop professionally and personally, but without the immediate pressure of a looming deadline, they tend to get pushed aside. For many of us, there's an internal drive to constantly prove ourselves, to be busy at all times. But true growth lies in carving out time for strategic thinking, learning, and building relationships. Focusing here can lead to tremendous progress, both in your career and in your personal fulfillment.

Next, we have Urgent but Not Important tasks. These often come from external demands, things that feel pressing but don't necessarily align with your goals. As women, we can sometimes feel obligated to address these because of ingrained expectations to be accommodating or helpful. But here's where the matrix gives us permission to delegate. By learning to recognize and minimize these distractions, you can better assert your boundaries and focus on what truly matters.

Finally, there are the Not Urgent & Not Important tasks. These are the distractions—the time-wasters—that don't add any real value to your work or life. We've all fallen into the trap of doing things out of habit or because we feel we should, even when they don't serve a meaningful purpose. The matrix helps you identify these, giving you the freedom to let go of activities that don't contribute to your larger goals.

Consistently using the Eisenhower Matrix will lead to a noticeable shift. You'll find that the stress of unnecessary tasks starts to lift, and you'll have more room to focus on what truly matters.

## Taking Back the Clock

Time blocking is an incredibly useful technique for women professionals, especially when you're trying to strike that balance between work and personal life after figuring out what tasks truly need your attention. Once you've made that distinction between what's urgent and what's important, time blocking becomes your roadmap—giving each task its own space in your day, reducing the mental fatigue of figuring out what to do next. This is especially helpful when you're juggling multiple roles, as many of us do, both in and out of the workplace.

Time blocking is simple in principle: you divide your day into specific blocks, each dedicated to a particular task or set of tasks. For example, you might block out a two-hour window in the morning for focused, high-energy work and reserve the afternoon for meetings or other collaborative tasks. It's about structuring your day so that your energy is directed in the most productive way possible.

This concept is particularly powerful because it acknowledges the unique pressures we face as women. Whether it's navigating workplace biases or internal expectations, time blocking can help us create a sense of control and balance. By pre-planning how we spend our hours, we become less reactive to the unexpected demands that inevitably arise, both at work and at home.

What makes this approach even more effective is aligning your time blocks with your natural energy levels. Every one of us has different rhythms, and identifying when you're at your most focused and creative can make a world of difference. Some women feel their sharpest first thing in the morning, while others hit their stride later in the afternoon. The key is paying attention to when your energy peaks and valleys occur throughout the day.

For example, let's say you notice that your energy is strongest from 9 a.m. to 11 a.m. That's when you'll want to schedule the tasks that demand your full attention—whether that's tackling strategic projects, problem-solving, or working through something that requires deep focus. When you align your tasks with your peak energy, you're more productive and effective without having to put in extra hours just to keep up. But as we all know, even with the best planning, life can throw curveballs. This is where the importance of structure comes in, but with an important twist—flexibility.

Time blocking is an incredibly useful tool, especially for women professionals managing multiple roles. It allows you to organize your day in a way that makes room for the unexpected while still maintaining your focus. By assigning specific blocks of time for work tasks, family obligations, and personal care, you create a flow that helps you manage everything without constantly feeling like you're scrambling. Think of it as setting a rhythm that helps you perform well in all areas, without the mental juggling that often leads to burnout.

For example, your mornings might be dedicated to focused, high-priority tasks—those that need your sharpest attention. Then, as the day progresses, you shift into meetings or collaborative work, where the energy of the team can lift your own. And by the time evening comes around, you've blocked time for family or personal care, ensuring those parts of your life don't get lost in the shuffle.

But here's the key: within that structure, you need space to breathe. That's where buffer time comes in. Buffer time, or those extra minutes between your tasks, is a tool that keeps things flowing smoothly, even when the unexpected happens. As we know, last-minute requests or sudden shifts can throw us off balance. By setting aside buffer periods, you give yourself the breathing room to handle these interruptions without feeling like your entire day has been derailed.

Buffer time isn't wasted time. In fact, it's your safeguard, allowing you to handle urgent, unplanned tasks while staying grounded. Whether you're dealing with a surprise work request or managing a personal obligation that pops up, these buffer slots can help you pivot gracefully.

In high-pressure environments, flexibility within your time blocks can make all the difference. It's a subtle way of reclaiming control over your day, ensuring that productivity doesn't come at the cost of your well-being.

But as we all know, technology is here to help, and it can be a powerful tool in managing this balance. In today's digital world, leveraging technology for efficient scheduling is a game-changer for many of us. With so many options, from calendar apps to task management tools, the ability to visualize your day and adjust your plan in real time brings a level of clarity that's essential. For women professionals, this can be particularly helpful when juggling the demands of work and personal commitments.

Think of it this way: using digital tools to create clear blocks of time gives you a roadmap for the day. It helps prevent the overwhelm of having everything jumbled together. You can designate certain hours for deep work, meetings, or even personal care, and when these time blocks are visible on your calendar, it's easier to communicate your availability. Marking time as "do not disturb" signals to colleagues that you're in the middle of something important, minimizing distractions and protecting your focus.

But what's equally important is reviewing how this is all working for you. As life shifts, so should your schedule. Taking a few moments at the end of the week to review what worked, what didn't, and where things can be improved allows you to fine-tune your time management. Maybe some tasks consistently took longer than expected, or you found that your peak energy levels changed. This self-awareness is what makes time blocking adaptable—it's never rigid. By regularly adjusting your time blocks, you stay in control and keep your schedule aligned with both your work demands and personal life.

When you do this consistently, it keeps stress at bay and ensures that you are working smarter, not harder.

## Boundaries for Balance

Following the practice of time blocking, one element that stands out is the importance of boundaries. When I started time blocking, it became clear just how essential it was to draw lines around my time to prevent burnout and ensure that I could fully enjoy my life outside of work. Gradually, I found ways to set effective, respectful boundaries that improved my productivity at work while preserving the peace I needed after hours. This approach helped me manage my tasks and kept my well-being in focus.

Setting boundaries is crucial, especially in a world where work can follow us home—sometimes quite literally. With emails pinging on our phones and tasks popping up at any hour, the lines between work and personal life can blur quickly. Boundaries are not just about managing time better; they're about protecting our mental health and well-being. This is especially important for us as we often balance multiple roles, including caregiver, colleague, friend, and family member, each demanding time and energy.

The impact of setting these boundaries is profound. Without them, work can easily creep into every corner of our lives, leaving us feeling "on" all the time. This continuous engagement with work can lead to a state of chronic stress and fatigue, which, if left unchecked, can spiral into burnout. Studies back this up. A survey by the American Psychological Association found that 56% of working adults reported feeling they don't have enough time for personal activities. That number reflects something many of us feel deeply: the need to protect our time for ourselves.

We often bear a heavier burden due to gendered expectations that subtly insist we be perpetually available or accommodating beyond our male colleagues. These expectations, whether spoken or not, can create an unbalanced workload that leaves you stretched too thin. When you draw a line and stick to it, you send a powerful message about your own priorities—showing that you value your work as much as your well-being.

Think of it like this: when you set firm working hours, not only are you prioritizing your personal time, but you're also making a statement about your boundaries. You're letting your colleagues know that you are fully committed during work hours and equally committed to recharging outside of them. This balance doesn't detract from your professionalism; it enhances it. You're showing that you can deliver quality work without sacrificing your personal life.

It's also important to recognize how these boundaries can improve your productivity. When you set clear guidelines for when you're available, you remove distractions and can dive deeper into your work during focused periods. I've found that when we protect our time in this way, we get more done and produce better-quality results. Communicating these boundaries with your team, whether through a quick chat or a simple note in your calendar, can nurture a culture of mutual respect. Your colleagues will start to see that when your time is respected, you thrive.

When it comes to setting and maintaining boundaries, communication is the bridge that makes it all possible. I've learned that being clear and assertive is necessary. The clarity in our words protects our boundaries and helps others understand our priorities and limitations. One of the most effective approaches I've seen work is to use "I" statements— expressing what we need without leaving any room for confusion or misinterpretation.

Let's talk about assertive communication with colleagues. Often, it's the straightforward statements that carry the most weight, like saying, "I give my best during work hours, but I need to disconnect after 6 PM to recharge." Notice how this language is both professional and personal. It reminds others that taking care of yourself is vital for staying effective. Setting boundaries in this way subtly reinforces a message of mutual respect and balance, making it easier for others to understand and support your needs.

Another approach that resonates well in a collaborative environment is to clearly state when you need uninterrupted time. For instance, saying something like, "I need to focus on this project, so I'll be unavailable for meetings this afternoon," is polite yet direct. It's an effective way to set limits without feeling like you're stepping on anyone's toes. Framing your needs in this way shows respect for the work process while protecting your own time and energy.

Creating and maintaining boundaries is about incorporating rituals and routines that help reinforce those boundaries. One of the most effective ways I've found to truly separate work and personal life is through what I like to call "boundary rituals." These small, intentional actions can serve as physical or mental cues to help us shift from one role to another, preventing the stress of work from creeping into personal time.

Take, for example, the simple act of shutting down your computer at the end of the workday. Pairing it with a short walk or even a cup of tea can signify to your mind and body that the workday is over and it's time to transition to your personal life. This small ritual helps us mentally reset, creating a clear line between the professional and personal. Similarly, starting your day with a calming practice, such as a few minutes of meditation or journaling, sets the tone for how you want to engage with your work that day. Over time, these rituals become anchors, keeping you grounded and helping you maintain your boundaries with ease.

When it comes to family, boundaries need to be just as clear. I've found that setting specific hours for work and communicating these openly with loved ones is crucial. It's not always easy, but when family members understand why certain times are reserved for work, they're more likely to respect those boundaries. Involving them in the process is even better. Have conversations about what works for everyone, and find compromises that respect your professional obligations while honoring family time. This mutual understanding inspires respect and builds a supportive environment where everyone's needs are acknowledged.

Of course, none of these strategies work without consistency. It's one thing to set boundaries, but the real challenge is maintaining them. Gently reminding colleagues or family members of your work hours or quiet times, when necessary, helps prevent those boundaries from eroding over time. Whether it's reinforcing the idea that evenings are personal time or reminding family members of a designated work period, consistency keeps everyone on the same page.

## Embracing Self-Care

Michelle Obama once wisely reminded us, "We need to do a better job of putting ourselves higher on our own 'to-do' list." And she's right. For many women, the idea of self-care often gets pushed to the bottom, overshadowed by work commitments, family responsibilities, and the day-to-day hustle. But here's the thing: self-care directly affects how we show up at work and in our personal lives. Taking the time to recharge through exercise, meditation, or even a simple walk helps care for our physical health while also protecting our mental clarity and emotional stability. Women, particularly those in high-pressure roles, can often feel like they need to do it all. The reality is that when we neglect our own well-being, it affects how we perform at work and how we engage with those around us.

In a world that still expects women to juggle multiple roles, self-care becomes an act of self-respect. It's about recognizing that we can't pour from an empty cup. When we're constantly running on fumes, our productivity takes a hit, and burnout becomes inevitable. But when we make self-care a regular part of our routine, it strengthens our resilience and keeps us grounded, even when the pressures start to pile up. It's like giving yourself permission to pause, to breathe, and to refuel—so you can keep moving forward with energy and clarity.

What's more, when women prioritize self-care, it helps dismantle some of the stereotypes that women must always be the ones who accommodate and overextend themselves. Taking time for ourselves sets a powerful example for both our colleagues and the people in our personal lives. It signals that we value our well-being and that we won't compromise it in the name of unrealistic expectations.

In addition to boosting performance at work, self-care plays a vital role in creating a more fulfilling and happier personal life. When we take time to focus on our emotional well-being, we regulate our moods and build resilience, which is key to tackling life's ups and downs. Simple practices like mindfulness, meditation, or even spending a few quiet moments with ourselves can help us stay grounded and manage stress more effectively. This emotional balance translates directly into healthier, more meaningful relationships with family, friends, and colleagues.

When we are constantly running on empty, it becomes difficult to show up for the people who matter most to us. But when we invest in our own well-being, we come from a place of emotional abundance. This makes it easier to support others without feeling drained or resentful. It's a shift from surviving to thriving—where you're able to give without sacrificing your own needs. On a more practical level, self-care can help prevent long-term health issues that often arise from chronic stress. By taking care of our physical health through balanced nutrition, regular exercise, and mindful relaxation, we protect our bodies from the negative effects of stress, like weakened immune systems or heart problems.

This holistic approach ensures that you can continue to thrive in all areas of your life, supported by a healthy framework of personal well-being. To start building a self-care routine, there are a few strategies that can make a big difference without overwhelming your schedule. These are practices I've picked up from friends, family, and colleagues over the years, and they've served me well at different stages of my life. With so much on our plates, we need practical ways to recharge that fit seamlessly into our lives. Here are some self-care strategies you can start today.

The time spent commuting—whether you're driving, taking the train, or even walking—can be transformed into a moment of self-care. Instead of passively listening to the news or stressing over work emails, consider using this time to practice mindfulness. Apps like Headspace or Calm offer guided meditations or breathing exercises that can be done in transit. This mindful practice allows you to reset your mental space, lowering stress and preparing you for the day or helping you decompress on the way home.

One of my favorite self-care strategies is what I call a "Power Hour." This is an hour, once a week, dedicated solely to something that lights you up—whether it's reading a book, working on a personal project, or indulging in a hobby. It doesn't sound like much, but carving out this time for yourself can be incredibly rejuvenating. By focusing on something that brings you joy, you step away from your professional role and reconnect with other parts of your identity, contributing to your overall happiness.

Another way to blend self-care with professional growth is by organizing what I call "Professional Development Lunches." Once a month, gather with colleagues or like-minded peers for a casual lunch where you can discuss a new skill, an interesting book, or a passion project. These meetups create space for both learning and socializing, while also fostering a sense of community. It's a great way to feed your intellectual curiosity while enjoying the company of others, making it feel less like work and more like a nourishing break from the daily grind.

Another simple yet powerful addition to your self-care toolkit is reconnecting with nature. Taking just five minutes to step outside for a quick walk or a breath of fresh air can work wonders for your mood and focus. These small nature breaks act like a reset button, allowing you to return to your tasks with a clearer mind and renewed energy.

If you're looking for a gentle way to start your mornings, try "Morning Pages." This practice involves filling three pages with whatever comes to mind—thoughts, reflections, even random ideas. Writing like this each morning helps clear mental clutter and brings focus to your day. It's a quiet, personal way to sort through emotions and set intentions, especially beneficial on those days when everything seems to be rushing by.

On the creative side, consider dedicating a bit of time to something artistic, whether it's painting, writing, or even a small crafting project. Having a creative outlet can be therapeutic, giving you a space to express yourself freely without expectations. These moments of creativity help you unwind, but they also bring fresh perspective to the workday, often sparking new ideas and insights.

For busy days, try micro-workout sessions. A quick, high-intensity workout, even just ten minutes of jumping jacks, squats, or a short run, can elevate your mood and energy levels. It's a practical way to stay active without demanding too much of your time, and it leaves you feeling ready to tackle whatever's next.

One practice that's easy to overlook but incredibly effective is a digital detox in the evenings. Set aside some screen-free time to wind down—maybe with a book, some journaling, or a meal with family or friends. This small shift can improve your sleep and help you feel more present, lifting some of the "digital fatigue" that can build up during the day.

Finally, regular emotional check-ins can be very grounding. Take a few minutes every now and then to assess where you are emotionally. This pause to understand your feelings and how they align with your day can help you make small adjustments to avoid stress buildup and keep you moving forward in a way that feels manageable. Each of these practices is a small but effective step toward well-being, helping you feel more in control of both your personal and professional life.

The journey towards a fulfilling life—both professionally and personally—is ongoing and dynamic, much like the strategies we've discussed. If there's one takeaway I wish for you, it's the understanding that small, intentional actions can lead to profound changes. Each self-care strategy, each moment spent defining your boundaries and priorities, adds up. I encourage you, starting this week, to choose one strategy from this chapter to integrate into your routine. Maybe it's setting a 'do not disturb' period on your calendar to enhance focus, or perhaps it's a daily five-minute walk to clear your mind. Whatever you choose, commit to it for a week, reflect on the impact, and then, perhaps, add another.

Remember, balance isn't about perfection—it's about making choices that support your happiness, health, and success. Take it one step at a time. You've got this!

# CHAPTER 12

# BEYOND THE DESK: EXPANDING YOUR HORIZONS

You know, Marissa Mayer, the former CEO of Yahoo!, once said something that really sticks with me: *"I always did something I was a little not ready to do. I think that's how you grow. When there's that moment of 'Wow, I'm not really sure I can do this,' and you push through those moments, that's when you have a breakthrough."* I find her words to be a powerful reminder, not just for our professional lives but for life in general. As women, especially those of us tackling demanding careers, there's so much truth in the idea that real growth comes when we challenge ourselves to step beyond what we're comfortable with.

For me, as I'm sure for many of you, there's often a temptation to stay within the familiar walls of work—where we've learned to excel, prove our worth, and keep pushing forward. But Mayer's insight reminds us that breakthroughs don't happen when we stay in that comfort zone. It's when we push ourselves to explore, to try new things, that we truly start to grow in ways that impact both our professional and personal lives.

## The Full Spectrum of Life

When you allow yourself to step into new, diverse experiences, you unlock creativity, reduce burnout, and start to build a more fulfilling life—one that's rich not only in career accomplishments but in personal growth too. And I get it—stepping outside the familiarity of work can feel intimidating. We're often faced with pressures to conform, to keep excelling at the pace we're used to. But when you give yourself permission to embrace new activities, you're expanding your horizons in ways that might surprise you. It's in these moments of exploration—whether it's learning a new skill, joining a community group, or diving into a passion project—that you discover strengths and passions you might not have realized were there.

You'll find that these experiences spark creativity and bring fresh perspectives to the challenges you face at work. Research has shown that creativity is closely linked to happiness and life satisfaction. When you immerse yourself in creative pursuits, whether it's painting, writing, cooking, or even gardening, you create space for self-expression, something that might be missing from the more structured, often rigid environment of the workplace.

For many women, especially those balancing the demands of work and home, these creative outlets provide a much-needed release. You know how it feels when the pressure builds up—the to-do lists, the meetings, the family responsibilities. It's easy to feel like you're being pulled in every direction. But when you engage in something creative, something that brings you joy, it allows you to step away from the constant demands and simply be. You enter a state of "flow," where time seems to disappear, and all that matters is the task at hand. This state of deep focus and enjoyment relieves stress and makes you feel more grounded.

This isn't about adding more tasks to your already busy day—it's about creating room for activities that bring you a sense of fulfillment. And it doesn't have to be grand. Maybe it's a new hobby, like taking a pottery class, or something simple like going for a walk in the park with your thoughts. These moments, however small, can make a significant difference in how you feel, reducing burnout and giving you the mental clarity you need to face challenges with renewed energy.

We often feel the weight of balancing multiple roles, and the pressure to be perfect in all of them can take its toll. By exploring personal interests outside of work, we can develop a more holistic sense of self. This exploration can be anything that excites you—whether it's learning a new language, taking up a sport, or simply engaging in something you've always wanted to try. These activities allow you to push boundaries in new, fun ways, helping you break out of the box that professional life might sometimes place you in.

The benefits of these activities don't stop with personal growth. By stretching your creative muscles and trying new things, you're building skills like adaptability and cognitive flexibility—traits that are incredibly valuable in dynamic work environments. Engaging in diverse activities outside of work feeds back into your professional life in ways you might not expect. You'll find yourself bringing fresh ideas, renewed focus, and a stronger sense of self to the table, making you more effective at work.

When we allow ourselves this freedom to explore life beyond our desks, we also become part of something bigger. Whether it's joining a community group, participating in a book club, or volunteering, these activities foster connections that offer valuable social support. And as many of us know, having a strong support system is essential for maintaining mental health and resilience, both at work and beyond.

When you think about expanding your horizons, remember that it is about enriching your life in ways that bring joy, inspire creativity, and ultimately make you more fulfilled in everything you do.

As we think about how creativity and diverse interests outside of work can enrich our lives, it's helpful to look at real-life examples of women who have embraced this mindset. One such example is Lisa Weber, a former president of MetLife's individual business, whose story highlights the power of stepping outside professional comfort zones and discovering balance beyond the office.

Lisa's career journey wasn't the traditional path you might expect. Having spent much of her career in human resources, she wasn't initially groomed for an executive leadership role. So when the opportunity arose for her to take on a significant leadership position, she hesitated. She wasn't from a sales background, and the new role was going to stretch her in ways she hadn't experienced before. But instead of staying in her comfort zone, Lisa took a leap, realizing that leadership was about far more than just sales expertise. She learned to rely on the strengths of others, a skill that helped her grow from being a manager to a true leader capable of guiding large teams.

What makes Lisa's story even more inspiring is how she balanced her professional growth with personal interests. Living in Manhattan with two children, Lisa made running a core part of her routine. She would rise early, sometimes before the city even woke up, and run an average of 43 miles a week. Running became a way for her to recharge, find clarity, and build both physical and mental endurance—things that helped her manage the intense demands of her role. Her passion for running led her to complete eight marathons, and she's training for more.

Lisa's commitment to running provided her with a way to de-stress while energizing her both personally and professionally. By embracing this activity outside of work, she found a way to stay grounded, stay strong, and stay focused on what really mattered. Her story is a reminder that engaging in interests beyond our professional roles can build resilience, unlock creativity, and create a more fulfilling life.

While stories like Lisa Weber's offer inspiration, they often highlight how rare it is for us, as women, to break free from the norms that seem to confine us. The truth is, expanding our horizons is far more challenging than we often acknowledge. These challenges stem from both external societal pressures and internal biases we carry with us every day.

Externally, many of us face deeply ingrained societal expectations, telling us that our primary roles are to manage domestic responsibilities, to be the caregivers, the homemakers. This "second shift," as it's often called, is something you might recognize in your own life—the way you transition from the demands of your professional day to the endless list of home duties awaiting you. These expectations eat into your energy and your time, making it difficult to pursue anything that falls outside of these predefined roles. Worse still, the skills we develop while multitasking and managing these responsibilities, such as emotional intelligence and problem-solving, are often undervalued in both personal and professional spaces. This creates a double-edged sword: we're doing so much, but our efforts and the skills we gain from them aren't always seen or appreciated for their worth.

Then there are the internal challenges we carry with us, which can be even harder to tackle. I've seen this in myself and countless other women—this constant feeling of having to prove our worth, especially in male-dominated fields. There's this subtle but persistent fear: "What if I take my foot off the gas? Will I be left behind?" It's this internal voice that tells us we must always be doing more, performing better, and showing that we belong. We're told to keep up, to outperform, and to do so without letting up. The result? We feel that stepping back to explore something as 'frivolous' as personal interests or creative pursuits could set us behind professionally. And that's not an easy fear to shake.

Another challenge many of us face comes from within—a subtle but pervasive bias where we pigeonhole ourselves into professional roles. We often feel like we have to live up to expectations that aren't really ours, driven by societal pressures or even self-perception issues like imposter syndrome. This can make us hesitate to step outside of our work or to try things that might seem unconventional or, dare I say, imperfect. And let's face it, that need for perfection can be exhausting.

I've spoken to so many women who feel like they have to prove themselves constantly, sometimes even in areas that don't truly align with their skills or passions. We get caught up in doing more, being more, and yet often forget to check in with ourselves about what truly makes us feel alive or fulfilled. It's like we're running a race but have forgotten why we started running in the first place. This self-imposed limitation keeps us tethered to work, overextending ourselves until we find there's nothing left for personal growth or exploration.

But here's where the shift begins: recognizing that alignment between personal and professional life is possible and essential. Many of us struggle with this balance because we've internalized certain beliefs about our abilities and our roles. We sometimes doubt that our skills transfer well outside of work. I've seen so many of us shy away from trying something new because we think we're not 'good enough' or that we won't succeed. And that self-doubt, that inner critic, can keep us boxed in.

When we allow ourselves the freedom to engage in activities that truly excite or rejuvenate us, we begin to recharge in ways that fuel both our personal and professional lives. It's like hitting the refresh button. It is about giving yourself permission to thrive in all parts of your life. When we overcome these biases and embrace a more balanced approach, we unlock creativity and fulfillment that stretch far beyond the office. And it's in that space, the full spectrum of life, that we find the energy and confidence to thrive.

## Finding Your Flow

This holistic growth that expands your full spectrum in life often starts with something incredibly simple: discovering personal interests that both relax and invigorate you. For Lisa Weber, it was the rhythmic pace of running that provided her escape and energy. For you, it might be the swirl of a paintbrush, the tap of a keyboard as you write, or the thrill of speaking before an eager audience. These activities allow us to explore creativity, which can sometimes feel stifled by the structured demands of the workplace. The beauty of having personal interests lies in how they help us tap into that creative energy, which can lead to breakthroughs—both personally, and professionally.

Another wonderful byproduct of having a personal interest is that it teaches us discipline in a way that's enjoyable. Think about it: when you dedicate time to something you love, you naturally learn how to manage your time better. You find yourself being more deliberate about scheduling, and that focus seeps into your work life. For women who juggle so many responsibilities, that sense of consistency can be empowering. Dedicating time to something that matters to you also means you're prioritizing yourself, a crucial part of avoiding burnout and staying productive.

To begin this journey, it starts with simple reflection. Ask yourself: what has brought you joy in the past? What activities once sparked your curiosity but perhaps got lost in the shuffle of daily demands? Sometimes, looking back at childhood passions can offer clues. Was it painting, playing an instrument, or even something as simple as walking in nature? Reconnecting with those activities can reignite that creative spark.

One of the most empowering aspects is to align your personal interests with your professional goals. When the things you enjoy doing in your personal time feed into your professional life, it creates a sense of harmony. For example, imagine you have a passion for sustainability and take up gardening or get involved with environmental advocacy groups. This alignment helps create a deeper connection between your personal values and your professional responsibilities, making everything feel more integrated and fulfilling.

At the same time, it's worth considering hobbies that engage both your mind and body. Physical activities like yoga, dance, or even martial arts are great examples. These kinds of pursuits do require focus, discipline, and creativity. They encourage mindfulness and mental clarity, which can help you manage stress better and think more clearly, both at home and in the office. The way these activities engage the body and the mind simultaneously can lead to bursts of creativity and innovative thinking, enhancing your performance in all aspects of life.

But remember, this process doesn't have to come with any pressure. One of the most important things to keep in mind is that exploring new interests doesn't have to be about immediate success or productivity. Give yourself the freedom to experiment and try different things without worrying about whether you're "good" at them. This phase of exploration— whether it's trying a new art form, learning an instrument, or taking up photography—allows you to truly find what resonates with you. By approaching it with curiosity instead of perfectionism, you might surprise yourself by discovering passions you didn't even know you had.

Additionally, finding activities that connect you with a community can be incredibly rewarding. Joining a group, whether it's a book club, an art class, or a local hiking group, gives you the chance to meet others with similar interests. These shared spaces allow you to exchange ideas, get feedback, and learn from different perspectives, all of which enriches your own creative process. It's also a great way to build relationships and expand your network in a setting that feels supportive and collaborative.

These moments of discovery and connection are where you can find new sources of inspiration, energy, and balance, all of which contribute to your success in and out of the workplace.

## Making Room for What Fuels You

Discovering personal interests that light up your world is just the start. The real question becomes: how do you actually make time for them? It's something many of us struggle with—finding that balance between our professional and personal lives, while still making space for the things that bring us joy. With a few small adjustments, it's possible to weave these activities into your routine in ways that feel manageable and rewarding.

One of the simplest strategies to start with is incorporating micro-engagements into your day. This means taking just a few minutes to engage in an activity that brings you joy or helps you unwind. For example, if creative writing is something you love, spend ten minutes during your lunch break jotting down a paragraph or a few ideas. If you're drawn to painting, keep a sketchbook handy for quick doodles or color experiments. These brief moments of creative engagement improve your mood and can help you reset mentally for the next task. Research even suggests that small bursts of creative activity can boost cognitive function, so these tiny pockets of time can actually make you more productive overall.

A helpful approach is to build flexibility into your schedule. Many of us try to stick to rigid timetables, but the reality is, life rarely follows a strict plan. Instead of getting frustrated when things don't go as scheduled, think about your creative interests as something you can fit in during flexible windows. Maybe you have a free half-hour in the morning or find yourself with unexpected downtime in the evening. By using tools like digital calendars or even just a simple to-do list, you can identify when and where you can dedicate time to your hobbies without feeling overwhelmed by your other commitments.

Another strategy that works well is creating a dedicated area just for your creative pursuits. Think of it as your personal sanctuary—a corner of your home or workspace that invites you to relax and let your creativity flow. This space doesn't need to be elaborate. It could be as simple as a cozy chair with a stack of books nearby, or a small table with your art supplies ready to go. What's important is that this space is yours, a reminder to prioritize what brings you joy, even on the busiest days.

But as you create this space and try to integrate new habits, it's equally important to practice self-compassion. We can be so hard on ourselves, especially when it comes to new ventures. If you feel like you're not making progress fast enough or your creative efforts don't look or feel perfect, it's easy to get discouraged. But here's the thing: it's not about perfection. Your creative journey is meant to be fun, exploratory, and fulfilling. Allow yourself to enjoy the process without worrying about the outcome. When you give yourself permission to play and experiment, you'll be surprised at how much satisfaction you find in the smallest achievements.

I've also discovered that a powerful way to stay motivated is by engaging a community in your creative journey. Whether it's joining a local workshop, participating in an online forum, or even forming a small group with friends who share similar interests, having that social connection can provide a sense of belonging and accountability. You'll be surrounded by others who are on their own creative paths, offering support, feedback, and encouragement.

## Embracing Community Connections

In expanding your world beyond work, connecting with a community is one of the most rewarding steps. We've often discussed the value of networks, mentors, and supportive peers in the professional realm, but this importance extends into broader community involvement too. When you step outside your immediate work circle and involve yourself in community initiatives, something remarkable happens. You begin to develop a set of leadership skills and confidence that you might not even realize you were capable of.

Women who take active roles in volunteer organizations, local clubs, or even online groups often find themselves in positions of influence and leadership. You're managing projects, collaborating with new people, and making decisions that matter—these are experiences that translate directly into your professional life. It's a kind of practice ground, but without the pressure that comes with workplace hierarchies or performance reviews. You're leading, communicating, and strategizing in ways that sharpen your skills, and you can carry this back into your career with greater confidence.

And then, there's the personal fulfillment that comes with community involvement. Finding something you genuinely care about, whether it's a cause close to your heart or a hobby you share with others, can be incredibly fulfilling. It aligns with who you are, and when your activities outside work resonate with your personal values, it brings a sense of purpose that reduces stress and boosts mental well-being.

When you think about getting involved in community activities, the key to long-term fulfillment is finding something that truly aligns with who you are. It all starts with reflecting on your core values and interests. What issues spark your passion? Whether it's education, environmental causes, or gender equality, taking the time to focus on what really matters to you ensures that the activities you choose will feel meaningful and keep you engaged. Once you've identified those core passions, finding a community or organization that aligns with your values becomes a natural extension of your personal and professional life.

At the same time, it's smart to think about how community involvement can support your professional goals. For example, if you're looking to improve a specific skill, like public speaking or leadership, you could seek out opportunities that help develop those strengths. Maybe it's joining a local Toastmasters group or taking on a volunteer role where you're required to lead projects or speak in front of groups. Aligning your community activities with skills you want to enhance can provide you with practical experience in a supportive, low-pressure environment, which is invaluable for both personal growth and career development.

Another important factor is time management. We all know how tricky it can be to balance everything, so it's essential to find community activities that fit comfortably within your schedule. You don't need to dive in headfirst—start small. Maybe it's an hour a week or even a monthly commitment. Gradually increasing your involvement allows you to manage your time effectively without feeling overwhelmed. This approach keeps things manageable and ensures that your participation is sustainable over the long term.

Equally important is the type of community you choose to engage with. It's worth seeking out inclusive environments where diversity is celebrated. These are the spaces where collaboration and fresh perspectives thrive, and where you can feel fully welcomed and supported. Women professionals often face biases in other areas of life, so it's refreshing to be part of a group that values your contributions and encourages innovation through a variety of viewpoints.

And if you're looking to extend your reach even further, don't forget about the power of online communities. The internet opens up possibilities to connect with like-minded individuals across the world, removing geographical barriers. Whether it's through professional forums, interest-based groups, or online volunteer networks, digital platforms provide a flexible way to engage with others while broadening your perspective and allowing you to learn from a global community.

## Learning for Life

As you start exploring new interests and stepping into fresh community spaces, it's important to remember that there's a powerful tool that can drive lasting satisfaction in life—the growth mindset. Think about it this way: just as we commit to developing our skills at work, life outside of our careers offers equally rich terrain for growth. Adopting a growth mindset can make every new hobby, skill, or interest a journey of discovery and mastery.

For women professionals, this approach to personal development is refreshing and transformative. A growth mindset nurtures continuous learning, helping us approach new pursuits with curiosity instead of caution. With this mindset, even an unfamiliar hobby becomes an opportunity. Suddenly, activities like picking up a musical instrument or learning a new language are avenues for broadening our skills and enhancing cognitive strengths like memory and concentration, which can benefit all areas of life.

This way of thinking also creates room for resilience. When we pursue personal interests with an openness to growth, setbacks become part of the process rather than a sign to quit. It's about allowing ourselves to be learners again, to enjoy the thrill of starting fresh, and to experience satisfaction in mastering something we care about.

The beauty of a growth mindset is how it allows us to connect the dots between seemingly unrelated areas of our lives. For example, imagine taking up a hobby like gardening. At first glance, it might seem like an activity completely separate from your professional world. But as you engage more deeply, you start to realize that gardening teaches you patience, resilience, and a keen attention to detail—qualities that enhance your performance at work as well. This cross-disciplinary learning is one of the most rewarding aspects of nurturing personal interests; the skills you cultivate in your free time naturally flow into your professional life, making you more well-rounded, creative, and adaptable.

What's even more powerful about the growth mindset is how it encourages us to keep moving forward, even when we hit bumps along the way. Let's be honest, trying new things is rarely smooth. There will be times when you feel frustrated or uncertain. But women who embrace this mindset understand that every challenge is a chance to learn. When something doesn't work out, you don't see it as failure; you see it as part of the process. This kind of resilience is essential for personal fulfillment and helps us remain agile and open to change in our careers. The world is moving fast, and the ability to learn, grow, and adapt is becoming more important every day. By developing a lifelong learning mindset, you are constantly discovering new passions and honing new skills that enrich every aspect of your life. Whether it's reading a book on a topic you've never explored, learning a new language, or simply picking up a paintbrush for the first time, these experiences keep your mind engaged and your spirit curious.

The key to making this happen is to start small and stay consistent. The idea isn't to overwhelm yourself with massive goals but to align your learning with what you truly care about. If sustainability is important to you, you might start by learning more about zero-waste living or getting involved in local environmental initiatives. By pursuing interests that resonate with your personal values, you're more likely to stay motivated and make real progress.

Setting goals, even small ones, can also help you stay focused. It could be as simple as reading a chapter of a new book each week or dedicating a weekend to trying something new. The point is to keep track of your growth and let it be a source of encouragement.

As you set these goals, make sure to explore areas outside of your immediate expertise. By deliberately choosing courses or workshops that span multiple disciplines, you open yourself up to fresh perspectives and creative approaches. Imagine someone with a background in finance deciding to take a course in design thinking. At first glance, these fields might seem worlds apart, but this interdisciplinary approach can spark new ideas. Suddenly, solutions to financial problems could emerge from design principles, offering fresh ways to address old challenges.

Your professional network is an excellent resource for discovering these learning opportunities. Chances are, you know someone who has embarked on a similar journey of exploring new subjects. Reaching out to peers for course recommendations or joining industry-specific forums can help you uncover hidden gems you might not have found on your own. Think of it as a collaborative process—just like exchanging ideas at work, sharing learning experiences with your network adds depth to your journey. In this context, earning becomes a part of a broader conversation, enriching both you and those around you.

It's also important to connect this personal growth with your professional goals. If there's a skill you've been wanting to develop, like leadership or public speaking, integrating that into your career advancement plans can make it even more meaningful. When you discuss these learning goals with mentors or supervisors, it demonstrates a proactive approach to both your personal development and career progression. It's a way of saying, "I'm invested in growing, not just for today's challenges, but for what's next." This commitment to continuous learning positions you as someone who is always looking to improve and contribute in new ways.

Once you've completed a course or workshop, taking time to reflect on what you've learned can deepen the experience. Keeping a learning journal is one of the simplest yet most effective ways to ensure that the lessons stick. Writing down key takeaways and thinking about how they can be applied to both your personal life and your work helps cement the knowledge. This reflective practice also creates space for future exploration. You might realize there's a skill you want to dive deeper into, or you may notice a new interest taking shape. The act of reflection turns learning into something dynamic, a continuous loop of growth and application.

Each of these steps brings you closer to a fuller, more balanced life and a career enriched by curiosity and constant discovery. It's not about grand gestures or major shifts, but the small, meaningful moments we allow ourselves to explore. Think about the impact of trying something new—whether it's an interest that sparks your creativity or a passion that simply brings you joy. These moments of exploration ripple into every part of life, renewing your energy and perspective in ways you might not expect.

So why not start now? Find something that excites or challenges you, something that lets you step out of the routine. Whether it's an art class, a book club, or even a quiet morning walk, give yourself the permission to explore beyond the usual. Let this be the beginning of a journey that adds layers to who you are and brings you a renewed sense of purpose and fulfillment.

So, go for it. Take that step and discover where it takes you.

# YOU'VE GOT THIS

We are living in both challenging and exciting times. On the one hand, the obstacles faced by women in the workplace are significant, but on the other hand, there is a palpable sense of momentum building around the potential for women to thrive and grow. The promise of women's potential is now coming into the spotlight in ways it hasn't before. According to the *Women in the Workplace 2024* report by McKinsey, women have made meaningful strides at the vice president and senior leadership levels since 2018. These gains are worth celebrating, but we must also remember that they are more fragile than they appear. There's still a lot of work ahead.

The path forward will require resilience, creativity, and a firm belief in the possibility of progress. As companies work to tackle deeper, systemic issues, we too must push forward with determination and tenacity.

Maya Angelou once said, "We may encounter many defeats, but we must not be defeated. In fact, it may be necessary to encounter defeats, so we can know who we are, what we can rise from, how we can still come out of it." Her words resonate deeply in this moment. The setbacks we face, whether personal or professional, are part of the journey. There's a certain power in realizing that our defeats do not define us. This mindset, this resilience, will be our greatest asset as we continue to break down barriers and redefine what success looks like for women in the corporate world.

I hope this book has been an ally for you, a companion that offers guidance as you tackle the complexities of the workplace with this mindset of resilience and growth. As we reach this important moment, I just want to remind you of something really important: your career and your future are entirely yours to shape. It's not about conforming to expectations set by others. It's about finding your voice, growing in your own time, and embracing every part of the journey—whether it feels triumphant or uncertain. Throughout this book, each idea and strategy has been a part of the larger picture, pieces of a puzzle. Now, as you stand here ready to soar, it's time to bring it all together.

One of the most vital parts of this journey is speaking up. Whether you're in a meeting, speaking up in a negotiation, or simply sharing your thoughts with a colleague, how you express yourself shapes how others see you and, more importantly, how you see yourself. It's not about being the loudest voice in the room but about knowing your worth and letting that guide the way you communicate. When you own your voice, you claim your space in the workplace, and that's where real transformation starts.

The next step is mastering the emotional elements that come with work and life. Emotional intelligence is a core part of thriving both personally and professionally. By understanding your own emotions, you build resilience. Attuning to the emotions of others helps you forge stronger, more empathetic connections. It's through this emotional intelligence that you create the foundation for meaningful, lasting growth, and you lead yourself forward with compassion and clarity.

When you continue to grow emotionally, it's just as important to build your financial independence. For many of us, money can feel like a source of stress or uncertainty. However, mastering your finances offers freedom and gives you the power to shape your life in ways that reflect your values and dreams.

This freedom is part of the bigger picture, but so is staying curious and committed to learning. Our lives and careers are constantly evolving, and by embracing lifelong learning, you open yourself up to growth in unexpected ways.

In this process of growth, whether emotional, financial, or intellectual, remember to celebrate your wins. So often, we brush off our successes, telling ourselves it's no big deal or that we shouldn't make too much of it. But those moments matter. Each achievement, no matter the size, reflects your effort, determination, and growth. Celebrating those milestones is about honoring your hard work.

As you rise, remember that none of us rise alone. The people around you, including mentors, peers, and allies, play a crucial role in your journey. These connections are about building a network that lifts you, challenges you, and supports you through every stage. When you're uncertain, they'll offer guidance. When you stumble, they'll help you stand again. And in return, you'll do the same for others. This exchange of wisdom and encouragement creates a community of strength where each person's progress contributes to the growth of everyone involved.

But success isn't just about reaching the next rung on the career ladder. It's about balance, too. And balance, as we've come to understand, involves finding what works best for you. Recognizing that caring for your well-being emotionally, physically, and mentally is essential for thriving in all areas of your life is important. When you take time for yourself and nurture your health and passions, you gain the clarity and energy needed to excel in your career and in everything that matters to you.

Reiterating these insights from the pages we've explored, I want to share some practical ways to turn these pages into a lasting toolkit. First, treat it like a playbook for specific challenges. As you move through your career, different situations will arise—whether it's negotiating for a raise, managing office dynamics, or building stronger relationships with your team. When those moments come, revisit the chapters that speak to those challenges. These sections are designed to give you actionable steps to help you navigate through, whether you're preparing for a tough conversation or working on presenting yourself in a new role.

Another way to make the most of what you've learned is by creating your own action plan. Growth happens gradually and with intention. Look back at the strategies that resonated with you the most and start building a plan around them. For example, if you want to work on your leadership presence, consider practicing one tip at a time, such as how you communicate or how you carry yourself in meetings. Try it out consistently for a month and see how it feels. The idea is to take it one step at a time, building confidence as you go.

When you actively integrate these lessons into your life, one thing is certain: growth is an ongoing process. It's not something you do once and forget about. That's why it's important to regularly pause, reflect, and reassess. Set aside time, maybe every few months or even twice a year, to pause and think about where you are. How are you doing with your goals? Are you seeing growth in the areas you've focused on? Do some strategies need tweaking, or do you need to revisit a particular section to fine-tune your approach? Perhaps the strategies on emotional intelligence or work-life balance could use a refresher. By checking in with yourself, you'll have the clarity to stay on track and make the shifts needed as you progress.

And remember, this is far from an ending; it's really just the beginning. What you've gained here is a toolkit that you'll carry with you for the long term. You now have what it takes to rise, to thrive, and to claim your place in whatever space you step into.

There will be days that feel uncertain, days when you wonder if you're headed in the right direction. When that happens, return to these pages. Let them remind you of your strength and potential. Because the truth is, you're capable of incredible things, and this journey is yours to shape.

Forging ahead, know that you're starting from a place of power: stronger, clearer, and ready to face whatever comes next. *You've got this!*

# ABOUT THE AUTHOR

Bidisha Banerjee brings a rich and versatile background in organizational development and women's leadership coaching. As a dynamic HR leader and accomplished career woman, she leverages strategic insight and data-driven methodologies to design scalable talent development programs and succession planning frameworks that enhance workforce resilience and drive sustainable growth. Her approach prioritizes leadership transitions, proactively builds a strong internal talent pipeline, and aligns development initiatives with organizational objectives.

A passionate coach and advocate for women in the workplace, she is dedicated to empowering talent, building resilience, strategic thinking, and career advancement through mentorship. Her approach extends beyond traditional development, driving transformation and promoting a culture of continuous growth and innovation. In her book, Bidisha combines her extensive experience with actionable insights, equipping women professionals with the tools they need to thrive in challenging work environments.